P9-CLX-477

Property of W. Springfield
High School Library

SCHIZOPHRENIA

Other titles in Diseases and People

—Diseases and People—

SCHIZOPHRENIA

Jane E. Phillips
and
David P. Ketelsen

Property of W. Springfield
High School Library

Enslow Publishers, Inc.

40 Industrial Road	PO Box 38
Box 398	Aldershot
Berkeley Heights, NJ 07922	Hants GU12 6BP
USA	UK

http://www.enslow.com

616.89
PHI

$20.95

PO 21727-04

5/8/04   Enslow

Copyright © 2003 by Jane E. Phillips and David P. Ketelsen

All rights reserved.

No part of this book may be reproduced by any means
without the written permission of the publisher.

Library of Congress Cataloging-in-Publication Data

Philips, Jane E.
    Schizophrenia / Jane E. Philips and David P. Ketelsen.
        p. cm. — (Diseases and people)
    Includes bibliographical references and index.
    ISBN 0-7660-1896-2
    1. Schizophrenia—Juvenile literature. [1. Schizophrenia. 2. Mental illness.]
    I. Ketelsen, David P. II. Title. III. Series.
    RC514 .P486 2002
    616.89'82—dc21
                                                    2002005380

Printed in the United States of America

10 9 8 7 6 5 4 3 2 1

To Our Readers:
We have done our best to make sure all Internet addresses in this book were active and
appropriate when we went to press. However, the author and the publisher have no control
over and assume no liability for the material available on those Internet sites or on other Web
sites they may link to. Any comments or suggestions can be sent by e-mail to
comments@enslow.com or to the address on the back cover.

Illustration Credits: © Corel Corporation, p. 19; Courtesy of Ian Chovil,
http://www.chovil.com, p. 15; Courtesy of the National Library of Medicine,
pp. 18, 21, 25, 27; Díamar Interactive Corporation, p. 41; © Digital Stock, pp. 44,
75, 86; http://www.btinternet.com, p. 50; The John F. Kennedy Library, p. 32;
Mark Clarke/Science Photo Library, p. 69; Photo Disc, Inc., p. 59; Sheila
Terry/Science Photo Library, p. 16; Simon Fraser/MRC Unit, and Main X-ray,
Newcastle General Hospital/Science Photo Library, pp. 51, 81; Wellcome
Department of Cognitive Neurology/Science Photo Library, p. 54.

Cover Illustration: Mike Bluestone/Science Photo Library, background; © Corel
Corporation, overlay.

Contents

SCHIZOPHRENIA

What is it? Schizophrenia is a mental disorder that is characterized by confused thinking and an inability to respond, communicate, or behave appropriately. Those who suffer from the disease may also see or hear things that are not there (a symptom known as hallucinating), or feel like others are out to get them (a symptom known as paranoia). This disorder is not thought to be progressive, but it is chronic and debilitating.

Who gets it? Approximately one percent of the population develops schizophrenia. It does not seem to be more prevalent in any race or within one sex. Schizophrenia very rarely appears before the age of fifteen or after the age of forty. Twin and family studies show that genetic factors play a role in who develops schizophrenia, but it seems that there may be an environmental cause, as well.

How do you get it? It is not known how someone develops schizophrenia. Research is currently being done to find causes during fetal development and early childhood. Some doctors think that a virus may cause the disease in some people who are genetically vulnerable. What is known about schizophrenia is that it is caused by changes in brain structure and function. Whether these changes happen during development or while the patient is growing up is not understood.

What are the symptoms? Symptoms of schizophrenia include disordered thinking, delusions, paranoia, auditory hallucinations, and psychosis. Many of the symptoms of schizophrenia are similar to those of other disorders or problems. These include drug abuse, head injury, brain tumor, and other mental disorders such as depression and schizoaffective disorder. Doctors must rule out these other causes and observe the patient for months before making the diagnosis of schizophrenia.

How is it treated? Schizophrenia is treated with medication and therapy. Sometimes, people suffering from schizophrenia are hospitalized during psychotic episodes to protect them from harming themselves and to allow them intensive therapy and medical treatment. Because the disease is chronic, most people who suffer from schizophrenia must stay on their medications and attend therapy sessions for life.

How can it be prevented? Because the cause of schizophrenia is unknown, ways to prevent it have not yet been defined.

Schizophrenia: The Monster That Steals Youth

1

"**M**y acne was just beginning to clear up when I started experiencing the first symptoms of schizophrenia," Ian said. He noticed that he was behaving differently when he fell in love at the age of seventeen, and could not even try to maintain the relationship. Although he had wished for this for such a long time, he just could not sustain the interest needed to keep his girlfriend happy. He had once been a very motivated, hard-working person with lots of plans and dreams, but he began to lose focus. "My mother says now that she noticed a change [when he was] around eighteen, that I lost all my ambition to succeed."

During his high school and college years, Ian became rebellious and very emotional. He stopped planning for his future:

I took courses that sounded interesting, smoked a lot of marijuana, and drank too much at parties. I was notably incapable of and uninterested in a long-term romantic relationship and, in fact, was very anxious in any kind of social situation. I doubt that any psychiatrist would have been able to diagnose schizophrenia at that point, though.[1]

Recognizing schizophrenia in the early stages is not always easy. The onset can be gradual. Ian explains:

Typically in schizophrenia, the last individual to realize they are ill is the person who has the illness . . . [you] lose your ambitions, your relationships, your possessions, and your skills . . . you can lose everything and end up a homeless person, completely alone in the world, and that is what happened to me.[2]

Ian did finish college because he was intelligent enough to do this with little work and very little ambition. But it was a difficult time for him because he did not understand what was happening in his mind. He spent most of his days sleeping and daydreaming. He had no idea what he was going to do when he finished school. When he found that he did not have a job after graduation, he decided to apply to graduate school. Ian had his first psychotic episode, which he describes as a nervous breakdown, in graduate school.

During the first year, Ian kept going to the student health clinic with vague complaints of not feeling well. He thought that someone was trying to poison him. The doctors there finally told Ian to see a psychiatrist, which he did. He ended up hospitalized and on medication. But no one told him what was wrong or what the medication was for—and there was no discussion of schizophrenia.

Ian remembers feeling confused during this time. He returned to school and tried to graduate, but things were not working out as planned and he was eventually kicked out because he could not finish his work or make himself go to classes. He moved out of his parents' home and began to travel and live in different places. Within two years, he was homeless. What happened during that time is not well defined. Ian says that much of it is just a blur.

Most of the time, Ian felt *paranoid,* or unusually worried that people wanted to hurt him, and had delusions. He was usually organized enough to rent a small apartment or a room in a boarding house. But in general, he had no money and felt hungry and frightened. He began to talk to an imaginary World War II veteran, who "told" him that the war had been caused by a virus. Ian believed that if people in the different countries had not gotten the virus, World War II would never have happened. Ian felt that he needed to tell this information to the world, so he went out into the streets to inform people.

He also felt that people were talking to each other about him and his theory. If someone came up to him on the street to talk, Ian felt that this person already knew him, even if they had not met him before. He thought that they knew about his World War II theory and that they were trying to argue with him about it. He did not understand why he was always getting into fights.

Ian deteriorated over the next ten years and began sleeping in parks and on the side of the road. He studied with a Tibetan Buddhist Lama and believed that he could easily become a Buddhist saint if the CIA (the Central Intelligence Agency—a United States government agency that gathers information) was not always after him and following him, watching his every move. But most of the time, he thought that aliens were going to come to the Earth and rescue him from all of his problems. They would eventually make him an alien, too, and he would marry an alien wife:

> I knew I was going to become an alien in 1991 because I saw a book written by Nostradamus entitled *3791*. I turned thirty-seven in 1991, so that obviously [was a] message to me. I had what are called 'ideas of reference,' where things are thought to have a particular meaning just for you. For example, a license plate on the street could be an important and appropriate message for me from the aliens.[3]

Ian was sure that the Earth was going to be destroyed and that he would live in a box that would float in space. He would marry a blue-skinned woman. The children they would have would be turquoise. Eventually, she would make him into a blue alien, too.

At this point, Ian was dirty, disorganized, tired, and broke. He had so many imaginary friends and imaginary enemies that he could not keep up with them. To calm himself down, he began to drink alcohol. Before he knew it, he was drinking all the time. He took a job in a Toronto department store changing light bulbs, but spent his salary on liquor and beer. He also got into trouble with the police.

One night, he asked the "aliens" to please transfer his mind to another body, one that worked better and that was not always being poisoned:

> When I woke up, still in my body, I became furious, and started breaking windows in the rooming house. Someone called the police, who interrupted my rampage, and I spent a couple of nights in jail.[4]

Part of Ian's sentence was that he attend sessions with a psychiatrist. But Ian thought, "Psychiatrists are only human . . . while I was almost alien and they wouldn't have understood what was happening so I never told them anything. I went to my appointments to stay out of jail."

Ian tried to kill himself by drinking several bottles of vodka at one time:

> I remember sitting on the ledge of a window on the sixth floor, wanting to jump but knowing that the aliens would have an open truck loaded with mattresses come by just as I jumped and when I actually saw such a truck weeks later, it only confirmed my conclusions.[5]

Ian was fired from his job and was drunk every day. He lived on welfare. "I could see the men sleeping on hot air vents nearby and knew that that was where I was heading," he says. "The aliens controlled everything that happened to me and I made one last attempt to argue against them."

Timeline of a Typical Patient With Schizophrenia

1. The patient exhibits less intense symptoms of schizophrenia. This is known as the *prodromal stage*.
2. Family and friends become concerned with the behaviors the patient is exhibiting, but the patient may not be able to understand or see that he or she has a problem. This lack of insight is called *anosognosia*—the inability to perceive the change in behavior.
3. The patient experiences a psychotic break and full-blown schizophrenia begins.
4. The patient is hospitalized or treated in an outpatient clinic.
5. Medication and/or therapy are prescribed.
6. The patient is released from the hospital or program once he or she is stable.
7. Monitoring of the patient continues for life.[6]

Eventually, he knew he could not live like that anymore. He checked into the hospital to be treated for alcoholism. While there, he took antipsychotic medication and was told that he was suffering from schizophrenia. Ian had a hard time accepting this and was very angry for a long time. But therapy helped him to understand it, and the medications helped his mood and took away the delusions. He worked with the counselors in his community after being released from the hospital and started to do volunteer work. He eventually started a full-time job.

His recovery was very slow, but Ian is doing much better these days. He has sustained some good friendships and is reunited with his family. He describes schizophrenia as a thief:

> I have a lot of unpleasant memories in which I've done things I now regret. It is difficult to know how much I'm responsible for and how much schizophrenia is responsible for. I think it is important for me to focus on enjoying life as much as I can and not dwell on the past. Life is a series of opportunities as you grow older, and I missed all of them.[7]

Schizophrenia is a disease of the brain that disables people, changing their lives and the way that they think. They become disorganized. Simple tasks such as bathing and paying bills are difficult. They hear voices that are not there. They may become para-noid. In addition, they may become depressed as they become more and more isolated from their family

After years of therapy and medication, Ian Chovil's life has improved greatly.

Many people who suffer from schizophrenia become depressed as they feel themselves lose control and become isolated from friends and family.

and friends. It is a devastating illness, but it is treatable. It cannot be cured, but those living with schizophrenia can now lead relatively normal lives. Patients can benefit from therapy, medication, understanding, and education. In addition, people without schizophrenia can understand the disease better through education and help to make those suffering from it feel less isolated from society.

2

History

Mental illness is as old as humankind. How a society treated a person with schizophrenia or other mental illness has been different throughout history and was dependant on the culture's philosophies and values. For example, archeologists have found ancient human skulls with holes drilled into them. The process of drilling holes in the head of a person suffering from mental illness was known as *trepanation*. It was thought by primitive people to release the "evil spirits" that lived in the mind.

The earliest accounts of mental illness come from the Egyptians, who did not feel that there was a difference between mental and physical illness. They thought that the heart was the part of the body that was sick when someone was suffering from mental illness. They believed that illnesses were caused by a loss of money, faith in the gods, or status.

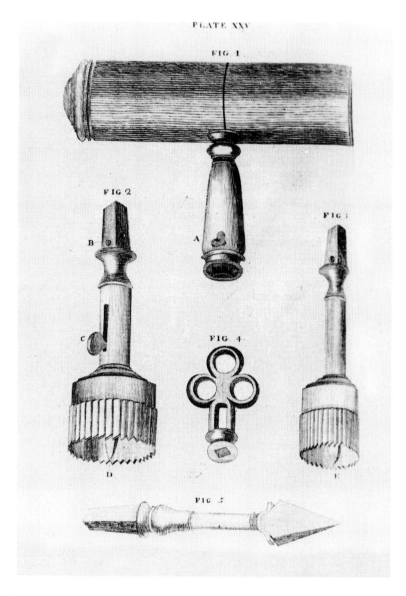

Primitive people in some parts of the world viewed trepanation, or the practice of drilling holes in a person's head, as a valid medical procedure. This illustration shows some equipment used in the practice of trepanation.

Their "cure" was to sit with the person and to talk to them about their thoughts, much like we do in modern therapy today. If the talking could not solve the problems, the Egyptians felt that it would be all right for the sufferer to commit suicide, because that action was not considered wrong in their society.[1]

Ancient Greeks and Romans had strong opinions on mental health, as well. The Greek storyteller Homer felt that the gods had taken the mind away from someone who was mentally ill and that because the mind was now gone, there was no cure. The philosopher Plato (c. 427–347 B.C.) said that madness

Ancient Egyptians thought that the heart was the part of the body that was sick when someone was suffering from mental illness. Shown here is an illustration of Anubis, the Egyptian god of the underworld.

was actually a gift from the gods and not a shameful thing. Those who suffered from it were closer to the gods and more creative.

Hippocrates (c. 460–380 B.C.) was a well-known ancient Greek physician who is called the father of medicine. Hippocrates felt that mental illness was caused by an imbalance in the body. It could be cured, he said, through exercise and an all-vegetable diet.

The Greek philosopher Aristotle (384–322 B.C.) felt that those who suffered from "melancholia," or depression, could be cured with music. Many people during these early times thought that cures could come from stories, humor and laughter, bright sunshine, herbal medication, and healthy food. There were some who believed repetitive activities like weaving or making baskets could calm the mind.[2]

After the fall of Rome, those living in the Middle Ages (A.D. 400–1500) had a very different view of mental illness. During these times, the general idea was that people who suffered from mental illness were possessed by the devil and that evil spirits lived in their minds. The approach then was to get the evil spirit or devil to leave. If this could not be accomplished, the mentally ill person could be burned or hanged.

Doctors tried many things to remove the "evil spirit," including bloodletting, or draining blood from a person, and laxatives. Nuns and monks took care of many mentally ill patients during the Middle Ages, so there were countless opportunities for *exorcism*, or a ritual performed to remove the devil from a person's body. Much of the time, the mentally ill lived in the streets or within the convents.[3]

The late seventeenth century saw changes in all areas of medicine, and this was when the practice of putting the mentally ill into institutions to remove them from the general community began. It was felt that if the patients could be cured, they could then be returned to society. But at first, sufferers of mental illness were placed in jails and hospitals.

The early hospitals were very inhumane—there were iron shackles for restraining the patient and chains to tie them to the walls of their cells, which were usually damp and without

Dr. Philippe Pinel was one of the first doctors to believe that his mentally ill patients were not morally defective, but were suffering from a medical condition.

21

fresh air. There was usually little sunlight and very poor food. Prisoners were dressed in straitjackets, which bound their arms inside their shirts so they could not use their hands. In some institutions, the mentally ill were beaten. The community did not feel that this was wrong because many believed that the mentally ill were weak and had allowed the demons to come into their brains, so they deserved to be punished.

Often, the mentally ill were housed in the same cells as criminals. The patients were believed to have committed the "crime" of abandoning their mind and allowing the devil to take control. The fact that these people were suffering from a disorder was not considered. The main thought was to blame the patient for his or her problem. Some women were put into these institutions because they did not listen to their husbands or because their family wanted their money. There was no real way to diagnose mental illness, so if a family member said that a person was sick, he or she could easily be committed to one of the institutions and never be released.[4]

The eighteenth century brought a more humane approach with the first mental hospitals and asylums. For the first time, doctors were assigned to care for the mentally ill and the patients were looked upon as medical cases. People called the physicians in charge of these institutions "lunatic-doctors" or "mad-doctors." Although they were trying, the cure rate was very low and doctors found that the asylums were becoming overcrowded. Many doctors tried different techniques to help their patients, but the majority of patients just received custodial care, which included a bed and food and water.

Salem Witch Trials

The Salem witch trials were a series of trials that were spurred on by the unusual behavior of several young girls in Salem, Massachusetts in 1692.

There have been many explanations given for how the Salem witch trials first started. What they all have in common is the starting point of the strange behavior of Elizabeth Parris, age nine, and Abigail Williams, age eleven, both daughters of prominent families in Danvers, a parish of Salem.

The strange behavior included blasphemous screaming, convulsive seizures, trancelike states, and mysterious spells. These are all symptoms of a psychotic state—a state that is indicative of schizophrenia, as well as a number of other problems, including the oft-cited explanation of ergot in Salem's rye supply. Ergot can lead to psychotic behavior due to chemical properties that are similar to LSD, an illegal drug that induces *hallucinations* (seeing things that are not there). Schizophrenia would be a simpler explanation because it is much more common, typically affecting one percent of the population, although it is less common in children under twelve years of age.

Regardless of cause, before the hysteria was over, twenty-four people had died. Some were hung in public executions, others died in prison, and one man was killed during torturous questioning. He was crushed to death because he would not accuse others of being witches.

While there is no concrete proof that the people involved in the Salem witch trials suffered from schizophrenia, it is thought that some people who suffered from mental illness were victims in the witch trial proceedings.[5]

In 1752, the Quakers founded the Pennsylvania Hospital, which was open and bright. The doctors there focused on keeping the surroundings clean and feeding their patients healthy foods. They separated the violent from the nonviolent and proposed "moral treatment" of the patient.[6] This attitude spread and Benjamin Rush, who is considered to be America's first psychiatrist, opened a hospital in Williamsburg, Virginia. He divided the mentally ill into two distinct groups: those who had general intellectual derangement, and those who had problems such as depression. Rush did not like to see the patients restrained, so he outlawed straitjackets and chains. Instead, Rush designed many gadgets to help the patient relax.

One such device was the tranquilizing chair. Patients were strapped in and their heads and bodies were held rigid. Rush saw a decrease in their pulse rate and a relaxation in their muscles. He improved upon this invention by creating the *gyrator*, a wheel onto which the patient was strapped and then turned upside down. Rush felt that when the blood went to the patient's head, it would relieve the congestion that caused the mental confusion. He also put patients in a circulating swing, feeling that the repetitive motion would calm them.[7]

This new approach carried over into the nineteenth century, when more emphasis was put on treating the patient with dignity and respect and supporting the idea that mental illness was in fact a group of diseases that needed to be understood. German psychiatrist Emil Kraepelin was the first to look closely at schizophrenia. He described one of the defining features of the disease as a deterioration of the sufferer over

Emil Kraepelin was the first psychiatrist to describe the defining features of schizophrenia.

time. He called it "premature dementia," and said that it occurred mainly in the young and made them old before their time. Eugen Bleuler, a Swiss psychiatrist, said that patients with the disorder could recover and function, but only for brief periods. He described this as a return from dementia. Bleuler said that those who could return to reality suffered from "split" (*schizo*) "minds" (*phrenia*). He felt that the disease, while coming on quickly, did not cause brain degeneration because the patient could be "normal" at times.

Bleuler also described the four A's of schizophrenia:

- a blunted *affect*;
- a loosening of *associations*;
- *ambivalence*; and
- *autism.*

Blunted affect means that the patients are less emotional than normal in response to an upsetting situation. *Loosening of associations* describes the disordered thinking. *Ambivalence* means that the patients cannot make up their minds. *Autism* describes a loss of awareness of what is going on around them and a preoccupation with their own thoughts.

While the research continued, the treatment community worked toward increasing the humanity of care for the mentally ill. American socialite Dorothea Dix was so appalled by the conditions in some mental institutions that she worked for over forty years to raise money. She opened more than thirty mental hospitals in the late 1800s. Today, some mental hospitals are named after her.

Dr. Sigmund Freud's work revolutionized ideas on how the brain functions.

In 1890, the United States government penned the State Care Act, which required states to provide their residents with mental institutions. The State Care Act also required that these state institutions provide a higher level of care than private institutions. The attitude toward the mentally ill was changing.[8]

The twentieth century brought with it the thought that mental disease was not caused by a failure of the person and was not a spiritual disease, but instead was caused by an imbalance in brain chemicals or a fault with the way the brain had been formed. Shortly thereafter, psychoanalysis became popular due to the work of Dr. Sigmund Freud (1856–1939), an

Australian physician who revolutionized ideas on how the brain functions. Freud's approach allowed the patient to explain life situations, fears, memories, problems, and stresses. The psychoanalysts would then look at the patient's childhood for explanations. This started the trend toward *talk therapy*, in which patients are encouraged to recount experiences in their lives and talk about their feelings to promote healing.

Many other new treatments also arose at this time because researchers were looking for a cure for mental illness. Neurologists and microbiologists started to examine the brains of those who were mentally ill and reported that mental illness was a disease of the nervous system, not a moral weakness. In addition, group therapy, electroconvulsive shock, and insulin shock therapy became popular.

Group therapy allows the patient to work with a doctor as well as other patients with the same problem. The feeling of community helps the sufferer feel less isolated from society. *Electroconvulsive therapy* (ECT) helps in the case of some mental illnesses, such as depression. Patients are hooked to electrodes and given mild but painful shocks to alter brain electricity. Both group therapy and ECT are still used to treat mental illnesses today.

Insulin shock is no longer used because it is dangerous, but for a short period of time in the 1930s, patients were given insulin in high doses. The chemical takes sugar out of the blood stream, which results in the patient going into shock. This did not appear to help patients much but was popular for a while, until a number of patients died. Some therapists also tried *hydrotherapy*, where they immersed their patients in water, sometimes for days. It was thought that the contact with water would soothe them. Other doctors gave their patients drugs to induce seizures, thinking that this could change the brain chemistry.

This was a time of great experimentation, with few positive results. The United States government put a lot of money into the research because many of the soldiers in World War I returned with mental problems. Doctors felt great pressure to help the veterans who had fought for their country, but the available treatments did not prove to be successful. During this time, a shift in medical education began.[9] Those who were studying to be doctors were now required to learn the basics of the newly emerging field of psychology. Asylums were becoming less popular as people began to learn of the conditions with which the patients had to live.

In 1953, the National Mental Health Association took many of the metal restraints from mental hospitals across the nation and cast a large bell to symbolize the change in treatment in mental hospitals. The bell is inscribed, "Cast from shackles which bound them, this bell shall ring out hope for the mentally ill and victory over mental illness."

One of the most commonly used therapies from the late 1930s through the 1950s was the *lobotomy*. Doctors would perform brain surgery wherein they cut the connection between the frontal lobes of the brain. This seemed to decrease the activity of the brain and calm the patient, but many were left with lost memory and intelligence. This treatment actually won the Nobel Prize in physiology and medicine in 1946, and the practice was not stopped until late into the 1960s.[10]

The early 1950s saw the introduction of tranquilizers, which calmed the patient, and tricyclic antidepressants, which decreased sadness and depression. But the most revolutionary medication was the antipsychotic chlorpromazine, commonly known as Thorazine, which was approved for use in 1952. This medication revolutionized the treatment of schizophrenia and is still in use today. It allowed many chronically ill people to return to a more normal life and started the trend toward releasing these patients from institutions. Although the drug lithium was discovered in 1949, it was not given to patients until 1970. It was found to improve the patient's mood during depression and decrease the levels of mania, or hyperactivity, during manic periods. Those with manic depression could maintain their moods much more easily.[11]

The year 1959 saw the introduction of the *Diagnostic and Statistical Manual of Mental Disorders* (DSM). Doctors were working to classify mental diseases so that treatments could be designed to address specific illnesses. The United States had founded the National Institute for Mental Health (NIMH) in 1946, and the research done there produced the first medications that could be used to treat some common mental disorders. The Food and Drug Administration (FDA) approved the use of the element lithium to reduce the symptoms of mania that came with bipolar disorder, once called manic depression.

The medical community was now more optimistic about its ability to treat mental illness, and this was reflected in the attitude of society. People began to feel that patients did not need to stay in mental hospitals for the rest of their lives, but could be treated and released. In 1963, President John F. Kennedy proposed the Community Mental Health Centers Act to design a national system to help the persistently mentally ill by treating them through outpatient services provided by the community. This was a revolutionary idea, but the Vietnam War sidelined the Act, because people focused on the war instead of other issues.

The 1970s saw the return of service members with mental problems and this caused many changes in the system, including overcrowding of state institutions and a push to find more medications and better methods of therapy. This also led to the development of "revolving-door patients," where the chronically mentally ill were discharged from hospitals only to return again and again. Many of these people became sicker, did not take their medications or go to therapy on their own, and even developed alcohol and drug problems, which made them harder to treat. The push to release the mentally ill from institutions continues—and this has had both good and bad results. This policy has contributed to the rate of homelessness, but it has also promoted the beginnings of many community-based programs. Today, the idea of being institutionalized for life is no longer common.

With the 1980s came the introduction of new medications and the increase in popularity of older ones. Tranquilizers,

In 1963, President John F. Kennedy proposed the Community Mental Health Centers Act.

which had been put on the market in the late 1950s, became the most prescribed medications in the United States for many years. Most people were taking them to calm their moods and help them deal with stress. It was quickly found that they were addictive, and many patients had a hard time stopping them. The selective serotonin reuptake inhibitor drugs, or SSRIs, were also introduced in the 1980s. These include the "wonder drug" Prozac. For the first time, people with mental illnesses such as low-grade depression found that they could be treated and feel better. These medications are extremely popular today and are now being prescribed for other mental disorders, such as obsessive-compulsive disorder and bulimia.

Currently, we are looking at medications as a way to help those who cannot function in day-to-day activities due to disturbances in brain chemistry. If a child is hyperactive, he or she may be unable to concentrate in school, complete tasks, or sustain friendships. Ritalin, a stimulant, can actually calm the child and help restructure his or her thinking. People who have suffered from a traumatic event are described as having posttraumatic stress disorder (PTSD), and may be prescribed medication to help them move forward and heal from the pain of the event. Prozac has raised the public awareness of mental illness and in some ways has removed its stigma.[12]

We have come a long way from the misunderstanding that once surrounded the care and treatment of the mentally ill. Drug therapy and counseling services have become more common, and many people with schizophrenia are leading productive and happy lives.

3

What is Schizophrenia?

In libraries, bookstores, and schools, tens of thousands of people under the age of fifteen will read this book in any given year. That means that several hundred people will read about these symptoms, never realizing that they are in fact seeing the future of someone they are friends with—or maybe even themselves. One day, probably five to ten years from now, what they read here may be happening to someone they know. It is a sobering thought, yet statistically evident. One out of every 100 people will develop schizophrenia, but we have no way of knowing who they are until soon after they first exhibit serious mental difficulties.

Misconceptions

A common misconception about schizophrenia is the belief that it refers to "split personality." While the Greek root word *schizo* does mean "split," it is a historical term and was originally derived from a splitting between the mind and soul. It should not be confused with the disorder psychiatrists call multiple personality. The two disorders have nothing in common on the psychological level, even if it might occasionally seem like the person who is suffering from schizophrenia is acting like "a stranger" and not themselves.

Another misperception is that sufferers are to be feared and can be violent. Because schizophrenia is not contagious, there is no reason to worry about catching it, nor is the typical individual who suffers from schizophrenia any more prone to violence than anyone else. Later in this chapter, we will address violence and schizophrenia in more detail.

Definition

Schizophrenia is a mental disorder that severely impacts how 2.5 million people in the United States think, feel, and act. It is a disorder that makes it difficult for a person to tell the difference between real and imagined experiences and to think logically. Psychotic symptoms are present during the active phase and may include two or more of the following (no single characteristic is present in all types of schizophrenia):

- *Delusions*—False beliefs that are thought to be true even though contradictory facts are present.
- *Hallucinations*—The seeing of objects or the experiencing of feelings that are not real.
- *Incoherence*—The state of being disordered, or not connected in a logical way.

35

History of the Name

Schizophrenia has always been with us. The genetic predisposition to schizophrenia is built into the DNA (deoxyribonucleic acid) of every one of our cells. The environmental factors, which are presumed to affect how soon or frequently people get schizophrenia, have probably changed over time, but we can trace the suffering of people with schizophrenic symptoms back as far as the beginning of recorded history. Still, schizophrenia was not described as a single affliction until Jean Pierre Falret, a French researcher, called it *folie circulaire*, or "circular madness," in 1851. This seemed to ignite a fury of disease-naming. Over the next fifty years, schizophrenia was repeatedly renamed and defined in slightly different ways:

- 1860—Benedict Augustin Morel, a French psychiatrist, calls it *demence praecox*;
- 1871—Justus Friedrich Carl Hecker, a Russian psychiatrist, refers to this disorder as *hebephrenia* (after the Greek goddess Hebe, who represented youth and frivolity);
- 1874—Karl Ludwig Kahlbaum, a German psychologist, describes it as twin diseases *catatonia* and *paranoia*;
- 1878—Emil Kraepelin, also from Germany, pulls these two terms together into one disorder, called *dementia praecox*, or "premature dementia"; and
- 1908—Eugen Bleuler, a Swiss psychiatrist, renames the disorder *schizophrenia*, which is the term we use today.

- *Catatonic behavior*—Behavior marked by a total lack of movement or response.
- *Flat affect*—An appearance or mood that shows no emotion; robotic.[1]

The five psychotic symptoms listed above are all indicators of *psychosis*, a severe mental condition characterized by a loss of contact with reality. *Neurosis* is a similar condition but milder—a neurotic person knows that he or she is ill, whereas a psychotic person usually does not realize that he or she cannot think or judge clearly. Psychosis is prevalent in people who suffer from schizophrenia.

In one sense, schizophrenia is hard to define; yet in another, it fits our most fundamental assumptions about mental illness. The break with reality that lies at the heart of schizophrenia is what we imagine and fear when we think about mental illness.

Most people at one time or another have wondered—or even worried—about going insane. It is just something that concerns us all. If we hurt an arm or leg, we can see the place that hurts and probably even do something to fix it. When it comes to mental disease, there is nothing to look at or feel. Therefore, we may feel useless and often hopeless. That sense of hopelessness can be one of the scariest things about mental disease.

Often in books like this, this is the point at which we would say that the illness is preventable if only you do something now. Exercise can help prevent high blood pressure, diabetes, and heart ailments; not smoking will help prevent respiratory illness. It would be wonderful if there were a cure for schizophrenia or at least a way to prevent schizophrenia, as in the examples just given, but there is not—at least, not now. While there is a lot of research being done on schizophrenia and mental illnesses in general, the best that can be done for people who suffer from schizophrenia today is to try to eliminate as many of the debilitating symptoms of the illness as possible. Even that limited amount of care is far better than what was considered treatment for schizophrenia just thirty years ago. The discovery of several types of medication, described in subsequent chapters, have allowed many sufferers to lead more normal lives.

Schizophrenia is not something that happens purely by chance, but it is true that there is nothing that can be done to prevent it. There are some very effective treatments for schizophrenia, but the newer antipsychotic medications have only been around for about a decade. One of the reasons that people are frightened by schizophrenia is that so little could be done to help victims until very recently.

Chapter 2, you read about how devices, seemingly out of a horror movie, were used on people suffering from schizophrenia in the futile hope that they might help alleviate the symptoms. It was not until new medications were developed in the late twentieth century that true hope for a relatively normal life was possible for sufferers. This subject will be dealt with in greater detail in Chapter 5.

Defining Schizophrenia

What makes schizophrenia hard to define is that there seems to be a number of types of schizophrenia. In fact, schizophrenia is one of the most disabling and puzzling of the mental disorders. Just as the word "cancer" refers to numerous related illnesses, many researchers now consider schizophrenia to be a group of mental disorders rather than a single illness. According to Dr. Daniel Weinberger, chief of the Clinical Brain Disorders Branch of the National Institute of Mental Health, "Schizophrenia is probably many different kinds of problems that converge on the same syndrome, not just a single disease."[2]

Who Develops Schizophrenia?

Schizophrenia is a chronic, severe, and disabling brain disease. It affects about one percent of the population, and that percentage is consistent in every country and culture in the world. Because approximately one percent of the population develops schizophrenia during their lifetime, more than 2 million Americans suffer from the illness in a given year. About 100,000 new individuals who are suffering from schizophrenia are diagnosed every year.[3]

Current research indicates a strong genetic link to the development of schizophrenia. For example, a person who has one parent with schizophrenia has about a 10 percent chance of developing the illness, compared with a one percent chance if no relative has schizophrenia. However, in the case of identical twins, one twin is 40 to 50 percent likely to develop the illness if the other twin suffers from schizophrenia.[4] While this is a very high percentage compared to the general population, the percentage of identical twins both developing the disorder would be 100 percent if schizophrenia were a purely inherited disease. That would mean that any time one twin developed schizophrenia, the other twin would develop it, as well. Because that is not the case, there must be other factors that determine why some people develop schizophrenia, but most do not.

Scientific studies have been done with identical and fraternal twins as well as with people that were adopted, and all agree that schizophrenia is influenced by, but not totally determined

Lifetime Risk of Developing Schizophrenia for Relatives of Sufferers

Relationship to Person	Chance of Developing Schizophrenia
Parent	1 in 20
Sibling	1 in 10
Sibling and one parent affected	1 in 6
Children of one affected parent	1 in 10
Children of two affected parents	1 in 2
Uncles and aunts	1 in 35
Grandchildren	1 in 28
Nieces and nephews	1 in 35
General population	1 in 120

by, genetics.[5] Some types of schizophrenia do not seem to be inheritable at all—certain studies have linked schizophrenia to environmental factors such as intrauterine trauma before birth,[6] poor maternal nutrition,[7] or even outbreaks of diseases like influenza (the flu).[8]

Although schizophrenia affects men and women with equal frequency, the disorder often appears earlier in men, who are usually affected in their late teens or early twenties. Women are generally affected in their twenties or early thirties. Schizophrenia rarely manifests earlier than age fifteen or later

Many homeless people suffer from schizophrenia. They are unable to deal with a working environment or schedule and feel isolated from family and friends. Eventually, they may find themselves with no money and nowhere to turn.

than age forty. While there are juvenile cases in children between the ages of six and twelve, the incidence rate is only 1/60 of the adult rate. Only about one person in 6,000 will be affected by juvenile-onset schizophrenia.

How Does the Schizophrenia Sufferer Act?

People with schizophrenia often are unable to express normal emotional responses or to behave normally in social situations. As a result, many are withdrawn and shy—feeling awkward around other people. Most individuals with schizophrenia are not predisposed to violence and are often ignored as a result. This can be surprising to many people because sufferers are often portrayed as dangerous and prone to violence.

Many homeless people suffer from schizophrenia, due to a combination of many causes. These causes include problems that can be remedied, such as an inability to deal with a stable working environment or schedule. The causes can also be difficult to fix, such as the difficulties of living with psychotic episodes—both for the sufferer and the people around him or her.

In the first chapter, we related the case of Ian. His story is similar to that of many people who suffer from schizophrenia. Despite being quite intelligent, he was not able to work for many years because he was not able to predict what he would do or think in the future. One of the most troubling aspects of schizophrenia for the victims of the disease is that they are aware, to a greater or lesser degree, that they are not normal. They realize that most people do not hear inner voices telling them to do unusual things, or have other signs of psychosis. As a result, it is quite common for the person with schizophrenia to gradually fade out of his or her normal relationships with family members, friends, and coworkers and, as was the case with Ian, end up homeless and on the street in their twenties. Cases like Ian's are common, but it is also typical that the symptoms of schizophrenia subside somewhat later in life so that the person regains a more normal life by the time they are in their late thirties or forties.

Violence

Two exceptions to the general rule that people who suffer from schizophrenia are nonviolent exist. One is that sufferers may be prone to violence when they are taking illegal drugs. Another is that sufferers may be violent if they are feeling paranoid. This is not surprising because most people are more prone to violence when drunk or taking illegal drugs. This is even more pronounced with people who suffer from schizophrenia because they have more trouble discerning between reality and their delusions when on drugs.

Many reports on Web pages listed herein, as well as the journal articles that are cited, give the impression that people who suffer from schizophrenia are virtually nonviolent. This is not exactly true and provides a good reason to read carefully. Because people sympathetic to the mentally ill generally write these reports, they do try to put the best face on schizophrenia. Generally, when they mention violence and schizophrenia sufferers, they say that the sufferer, when properly medicated and

People who suffer from schizophrenia may become more prone to violence while under the influence of alcohol or drugs.

not using illegal drugs, is less violent than the average citizen. The flaw with this is that people who suffer from schizophrenia use drugs at a higher rate than the average person. This causes them, on average, to be more prone to violence. Several things can lead to violence with people who suffer from schizophrenia. They are:

- an antisocial personality type;
- delusions;
- hallucinations;
- drug or alcohol use;
- not taking prescribed medications;
- indifference toward the victim (people who suffer from schizophrenia are more likely not to know the victim of their violence); [9] and
- paranoid schizophrenia.[10]

People who are paranoid think that everyone is out to get them, which often makes them angry and violent. In the case of people who suffer from paranoid schizophrenia, it is even worse because they also have psychotic symptoms that can make them do rash and often mean things. They may not always perceive harmless actions as safe, and may put others at risk.

Despite having said all this, it is still important to keep in mind that a person suffering from schizophrenia will typically not act in a dangerous or destructive way as long as he or she is taking medication. And even when unmedicated, the more typical response is to become shy and withdrawn, rather than violent.

Summation

People with schizophrenia often suffer terrifying symptoms, such as hearing internal voices not heard by others, or believing that other people are reading their minds, controlling their thoughts, or plotting to harm them. These symptoms may leave them fearful and withdrawn. Their speech and behavior can be so disorganized that they may be incomprehensible or frightening to others. Available treatments can relieve many symptoms, but most people with schizophrenia continue to suffer some symptoms throughout their lives. In fact, it has been estimated that no more than one in five individuals recovers completely from schizophrenia.

The exact cause of schizophrenia is unknown. There are various theories to explain the development of this disorder. Genetic factors play a role, as close relatives of a person with schizophrenia are more likely to develop the disorder. Psychological and social factors, such as disturbed family relationships, may also play a role in development, especially as a trigger for onset of the symptoms.

4

Diagnosing Schizophrenia

I n the last chapter, schizophrenia was defined and its symptoms were described. That description allows mental health professionals to make a more accurate assessment as to whether a patient suffers from schizophrenia. The mental health professional's decision on the patient's mental status can affect the rest of the patient's life. Therefore, the mental health worker has to have definitive criteria to use. These criteria are from a task force of the American Psychiatric Association, which developed a diagnostic system for mental illness that is widely used in North America. The results of its work are published in a handbook called *The Diagnostic and Statistical Manual of Mental Disorders* (DSM). The fourth and most current version (DSM-IV) was published in 1994. The section pertaining to schizophrenia is in the appendix at the end of the DSM-IV. In other countries, a slightly different version is used. It is called the *International Classification of Disease*, or ICD-10. Basically, the criteria used in both are the same, although the amount of time that the symptoms need to be exhibited differs.

The Five Types of Schizophrenia

There are five recognized types of schizophrenia. They are:
- Catatonic
- Paranoid
- Disorganized
- Undifferentiated
- Residual[1]

Currently, there is no simple lab test to make a diagnosis of schizophrenia, although a few possibilities might be on the market soon.[2] Therefore, a diagnosis is based on the symptoms—what the person says and what the doctor observes. To reach a diagnosis of schizophrenia, other possible causes, such as drug abuse, epilepsy, brain tumor, thyroid or other metabolic disturbances, as well as other physical illnesses that have symptoms like schizophrenia must be ruled out. This is because many other diseases and habits—like chronic drug abuse—can mimic the symptoms of schizophrenia. Schizophrenia must also be clearly differentiated from bipolar (manic-depressive) disorder. The two disorders often appear with the same symptoms. Some patients show the symptoms of both schizophrenia and manic depression. This condition is termed *schizoaffective disorder.*

The simple test referred to above concerns a new computerized test developed at the University of British Columbia in Vancouver by Peter Liddle, a psychiatrist specializing in brain imaging. His test uses a neural network to analyze the brain scans of patients, looking for telltale characteristics in cerebral blood flow. "One of the big challenges with schizophrenia is the diagnosis. It can take several years for it to be made clear," says Liddle. "Being able to make a reliable diagnosis early can help to optimize the outcome."[3] Having an early-detection test like this available would be a wonderful benefit because most of the permanent damage to people who suffer from schizophrenia occurs early in the course of the disease, before they have been diagnosed by the methods currently available. While it would not be feasible to screen everyone using an expensive medical test like this, it would be possible to use it on people at greater risk for getting the disease, such as relatives of people that already have schizophrenia.

Ian, the man in the case study in Chapter 1, has this to say:

> Delays in treating the first psychotic episode, subsequent episodes and delays in their treatment, essentially cause irreparable brain damage, and the individual becomes more disabled, and less able to enjoy life. They also require increasingly expensive supports and services to live in the community.[4]

Another early test for schizophrenia that is in development is a blood test that also takes advantage of a difference that might exist between the blood of people with schizophrenia and the rest of the population. A statistical analysis done by

Diagnosing Schizophrenia Through Blood Tests?

Developing a blood test to diagnose schizophrenia would make things easier on doctors and on the patients and their families. But all blood tests used by doctors must be extremely accurate because it would be terrible to diagnose someone with a disease that they do not have. Recently, a group of doctors in Israel reported an interesting way to diagnose schizophrenia by a simple blood test. Hopefully, this test will prove to be accurate. The doctors were looking for the dopamine receptor, which is found in the brain. People who suffer from schizophrenia are known to have higher numbers of dopamine receptors in their brains than people without the disease. The researchers took blood from fourteen schizophrenia sufferers and compared it to blood from people who do not have schizophrenia. What they found was interesting:

If dopamine receptors are found in the brain, how could the doctors find them in the blood? For an unknown reason, white blood cells have this receptor, as well. The researchers found that the dopamine receptors on white blood cells are higher in people who suffer from schizophrenia, just like it is in the brain. Because blood cells are so easy to get by drawing blood, measuring the number of dopamine receptors on the white blood cell would be cheap, fast, simple, and almost painless. Early diagnosis could be very beneficial to the patient, so many doctors are hoping this test will prove to be accurate.[5]

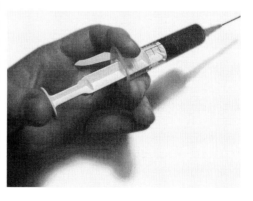

Dopamine research is becoming increasingly more important in the study of schizophrenia.

researchers in Israel showed that the blood of patients with schizophrenia contains, on average, 3.6 times more of a certain type of messenger RNA. Messenger RNA is the material found in the cells that tells them what type of protein to make. The increased messenger RNA in people who suffer from schizophrenia is for dopamine receptors. Dopamine receptors function by taking up the chemical dopamine into brain cells (neurons). In schizophrenia sufferers, there seems to be a large amount of messenger RNA for a dopamine receptor of a particular kind, called D3, more than is found in the blood of healthy people.[6] Unfortunately, it will be years before this test can be widely available because doctors have to be very careful to make sure that it is an accurate test. It would be terrible for a patient to be diagnosed with schizophrenia if they did not have this condition.

As was mentioned in the last chapter, people who suffer from schizophrenia commit suicide at a much higher rate than the general population does. In fact, one out of every six schizophrenia sufferers will end up killing him- or herself. This is another reason to focus on earlier diagnosis. Growing evidence suggests that the earlier therapy is begun, the better a patient's outcome will be. According to Dr. Richard J. Wyatt, chief of the Neuropsychiatry Branch of the National Institute of Mental Health, St. Elizabeth's Hospital, Washington, D.C. immediate antipsychotic therapy after the first episode of schizophrenia positively affects outcomes.[7]

Typically when diagnosing a patient with possible psychological or brain problems, the health care worker will use the DSM-IV criteria. The first step is taking a patient history that involves talking to the patient to assess his or her current mental status, talking to the family to get a patient history, and usually some psychological testing. Because one of the main determinants on whether the patient has schizophrenia or not is how long the symptoms have been occurring, the patient history is very important. If the lesser signs of schizophrenia have been present for six months or more, and greater signs have been present for a month or longer—then the diagnosis of schizophrenia is made.

Prodromal Stage

The word "prodrome" comes from the ancient Greek word *prodromos*, which means something that occurs before another event—in this case, the onset of schizophrenia. The prodrome is of little value to the patient, but is very interesting to researchers because it might allow them to predict schizophrenia better in the future. The prodromal stage is usually more than a few weeks long and can be interpreted as being more than five years long in some cases. It is marked by the same symptoms as schizophrenia, but not as severe.

Schizophrenia, as mentioned before, has very similar symptoms to a great number of other disorders or problems. Before a diagnosis of schizophrenia can be established, those other possibilities have to be ruled out. These include drug abuse, head injury, brain tumor, and other mental disorders such as depression and schizoaffective disorder. Although the cause of schizophrenia has not yet been identified, recent research suggests that schizophrenia involves problems with brain chemistry and brain structure. Scientists are currently investigating viral infections that occur early in life, mild brain damage from complications during birth, and genetic predisposition as possible cofactors.

If the patient seems to be suffering from schizophrenia after these tests, then medical tests are done to confirm the diagnosis. Tests used in this manner include MRI (magnetic resonance imaging), CT (computed tomography) scan, PET (positron emission tomography) scan, and EEG (electroencephalogram). These tests, by themselves do not make the diagnosis of schizophrenia but must be taken into account with patient history and observation of the patient's behavior.

No matter what happens during the first visit to the health care provider, the diagnosis of schizophrenia usually takes a long time. According to the DSM-IV, there needs to be a six-month history of psychotic symptoms just to be sure that it really is schizophrenia. This is because it can be a very difficult

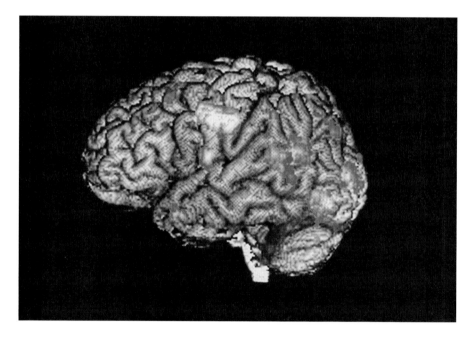

One of the most common tests used in diagnosing schizophrenia is the PET (positron emission tomography) scan. Shown in this PET scan is the left side of the brain of a person who is experiencing hallucinations due to schizophrenia.

diagnosis to make—the symptoms necessary for diagnosis often go unrecognized until the illness is advanced. There are also many differences among individuals in the way in which symptoms present themselves. Most doctors, well aware of the stigma that still surrounds this illness, do not like to voice their suspicions until they are quite sure that this diagnosis is correct.

Complicating Factors for Diagnosis

If any of the following are present in a person's history, diagnosing schizophrenia is even more difficult:

- insidious (slow) onset (schizophrenia often develops over the course of years and for that reason can be very difficult to perceive on a day-to-day basis);
- neurological soft signs (poor motor coordination, balance, or touch discrimination; often related to poor visual-motor coordination);
- past psychiatric history;
- history of violence;
- long duration of first illness;
- emotional blunting (very little emotion displayed by the patient);
- social withdrawal; or
- poor psychosexual functioning (integration of the mind and body in matters of sexual acts).[8]

Recently, standardized forms have become available for self-testing on the Internet. People who suspect that they might be suffering from schizophrenia have accessed these sites

Property of W. Springfield
High School Library

in the hope of taking these tests to arrive at a diagnosis. But it is imperative to understand that only a qualified health care professional can truly diagnose a person with schizophrenia.

Many people who are in the early stages of schizophrenia begin to act strangely. Be sure to tell a parent or teacher if you see someone you know exhibiting the warning signs. A large amount of progress can be made in treating this disorder if it is diagnosed early.

5

Treatment of Schizophrenia

Methods of treating schizophrenia have improved drastically over the past ten years mainly because of the introduction of new medications, but also due to a better understanding of the role the therapist, as well as the patient and the family, can play in healing the patient. Let us walk through a typical course of treatment from the first psychotic episode to the resolution of symptoms.

Allison is seventeen years old and about to leave her home to start college. She is anxious and worried that she will not do well in her classes and afraid that she will not make friends. She has noticed recently that she spends a lot of time alone and that she is feeling sad, but she thinks this is just due to her fear of leaving her familiar surroundings and starting something new. Immediately after starting school, Allison begins to spend a lot of time alone in the library or in her dorm room.

She does not want to go out or to see anyone. She only leaves to go to class. She begins to have thoughts that frighten her and seem out of her control. She starts to hear voices while she reads her textbooks. Two months later, she has her first psychotic episode, in which she cannot concentrate on other people or on her studies. She is unaware of time passing or of things going on around her. She cannot eat or sleep—she simply sits in the corner of her room, listening to voices in her head.

Allison is taken home by her parents, who decide to send her to a psychiatric hospital. She is immediately treated with both medications and therapy. Allison recovers well and is released in three weeks. Now, both she and her family educate themselves on schizophrenia while she continues to take medications and to see her therapist. Within a year, she is back in school and doing well.

Allison is lucky to have received such good care. It is believed that the earlier a patient is treated after their first psychotic episode, the less likely he or she is to suffer another one. The *prognosis,* or predicted course of the disease, is much better in people who are diagnosed right away and given adequate treatment. It is sometimes difficult for doctors to make the right choice on the course of medical care. Currently, there are several medications and many different types of counseling available. Some will work for one patient where they would not work for another. In general, treatment can be a course of trial and error, and both the doctor and the patient must explore all the options.

Medications

None of the medications used today can cure schizophrenia, but in most cases, they can make the disease much less devastating. Medications currently available to treat schizophrenia are called *antipsychotics,* and can be broken down into two basic categories: the *neuroleptics,* which are the older medications; and the *atypicals,* which are the newer medications. The neuroleptics have been used since the early 1950s to treat patients with schizophrenia, and they work quite well for many patients. The atypicals are considered better than the older medications because they have fewer side effects and they seem to work for patients who did not respond to the older medications. It is important to remember that different people respond to neuroleptic and atypical medications in different ways. Doctors have much to consider when choosing a medication, such as:

- the sex and weight of the patient;
- the patient's health;
- the age of the patient;
- the severity of the patient's symptoms; and
- how many psychotic episodes the patient has experienced.[1]

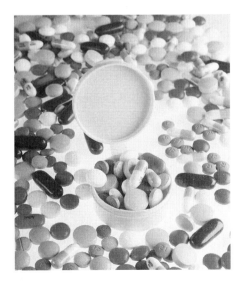

Neuroleptics and atypicals are the two types of antipsychotic medications used to treat schizophrenia.

Some patients are treatment-resistant, which means that no medication seems to help them. This happens mostly in people who have not been diagnosed quickly enough and have had many psychotic episodes. This can be quite common because the sicker the patients become, the more they pull away from their friends and family, so there is less chance of getting help. When they finally do see a doctor, they may not respond to medications at all.[2] Sometimes the patient gets help right away, but because they do not want to admit to themselves that they suffer from schizophrenia, they stop taking their medications and stop going to therapy. This can cause a relapse in symptoms and bring on a psychotic episode. Studies have shown that the main reason patients suffer a relapse is because they stopped taking their medication. For unknown reasons, this can make them harder to treat in the future.[3]

It is not always easy to take patients off a medication and start them on a new one. Doing this can increase the risk of a psychotic episode. Many doctors use a crossover method, wherein they will slowly decrease the amount of medication the patient is currently on while adding the new medication. This seems to work well in most cases, resulting in a decrease in the amount of psychosis the patient experiences while changing medications. In addition, patients who start drug therapy may have a desire to stop. The treating physician has a responsibility to keep the person on the medication to prevent the progression of the disease. It is thought that some patients should never stop taking their medications, while others can.

Monitoring of Antipsychotic Medications

Sometimes, it is important to measure the level of a medication in the blood on a regular basis to make sure the patient is benefiting from the treatment. This is called *therapeutic drug monitoring.* The doctor will ask that the patient come into the office a few times a year and blood is drawn and sent to the laboratory. There are a few reasons to do this. One is that the medication can be poisonous to the body, so the doctor wants to make sure the patient is not taking too much. Another is to make sure the patient is absorbing the medication well.

In the case of medication for schizophrenia, doctors may choose to do therapeutic drug monitoring to make sure the patient is taking the medication. It is very common for patients with schizophrenia to forget to take their medication because of their disordered thinking. In addition, some schizophrenia sufferers do not like to take their medication because it makes them feel sleepy or fuzzy. Many patients do not take it because they will not admit that they are sick. So psychiatrists may ask the nurse to draw blood from the patient during a visit, sort of like a "pop quiz" to see if the patient is taking the medication. If they find that the medication levels are low, they will counsel the patient on staying on the medications.

Deciding when and how to remove a patient with schizophrenia from drug treatment is very tricky and requires the help of a therapist along with step-by-step decreases over time. In some cases, when the patient stops taking the medication, he or she may become suicidal. For this reason, most doctors do not offer the hope of ending drug therapy and most schizophrenia sufferers will take medication for their entire lives.[4]

Let us look at the medications, how they work, and how they make the patient feel.

Neuroleptics

Neuroleptic medications include haloperidol and chlorpromazine. They are very effective in decreasing the incidence of the positive symptoms associated with schizophrenia and can have the patient feeling better within a few days. They are cheaper than the newer medications and, for this reason alone, can be the medication of choice during the first psychotic episode. However, they have some very unpleasant side effects. Mostly, users complain of being sleepy and "foggy." They do not feel themselves and lack emotion and creativity. In addition, they may deal with weight gain, blurry vision, constipation, dry mouth, and feeling faint.

But the worst side effects are called *extrapyramidal symptoms*, or EPS. These include acute *dystonia*, a continual stiffness in the jaw and neck, and *akathisia*, feelings of restlessness, muscle quivering, and an inability to sit still. Some patients can later display the symptoms of *tardive dyskinesia*, a distinctive condition in which the movement of their face and limbs cannot be controlled. Sufferers will have repetitive twitching of the mouth or blinking of the eyes and their knees may wiggle up and down.[5] Tardive dyskinesia is a side effect most patients want to avoid because it can become permanent, continuing long after the medication has been stopped. It will appear in 15 percent of all patients within the first three months of taking the medication. The onset of tardive dyskinesia is slow because it is caused by changes in the brain structure.

Neuroleptics work by blocking the action of a very common chemical in the brain called *dopamine*, which is a neurotransmitter that is used by brain cells to send signals to other cells in the body. People who suffer from schizophrenia may be too sensitive to dopamine in some areas of the brain. For this reason, neuroleptics may work better for the patients who are abnormally sensitive to this compound.[6]

Mainly, neuroleptics are administered as pills given a couple of times a day. In some patients, though, they may be given by injection. Sometimes the medications are given as a depot injection. This means that the medication is administered only once, into the muscle, where it is stored and used by the body over the next two to three weeks. Depot injections are used in patients who are not good at remembering to take their medications and are sometimes given to those experiencing their first psychotic episode.[7] These injections ensure that a steady dose of the drug is delivered to the brain at all times.

Atypical Medications

In many cases, the atypical medications are a better course of treatment because they have fewer side effects than the neuroleptics. While someone who is newly diagnosed with schizophrenia may be put on the neuroleptics initially, the doctor usually tries to switch them over to the newer drugs. The atypicals include risperidone, clozapine, and olanzapine. Risperidone is the medication most often chosen in the treatment of schizophrenia in the United States and it works well in most patients.

Clozapine is the first atypical introduced and it works on the most patients, including those that have not responded to other medications. The drawbacks in using clozapine are that it is very expensive, costing as much as $16 per day; and that in some cases, it may cause a disease called *agranulocytosis*. People who develop agranulocytosis have a very low level of white blood cells circulating in their body and can no longer fight infection. If the white cell count goes too low, patients may become very sick or die from an infection. While this only occurs in one or two patients out of every 100, it can be fatal, so patients are monitored or tested every two weeks.[8]

The side effects of the atypicals are easier for the patient to handle. These side effects include weight gain and sleepiness along with hypersalivation (drooling). In addition, it is thought that the atypicals can prevent relapse much better than the neuroleptics, although more studies need to be done to confirm this. Because the side effects are not as bad with these medications, patients tend to take them more reliably.

This could contribute to their ability to prevent relapse. Atypicals are administered as pills and there are currently no depot injections of these medications on the market.

Most patients are started at a low dose of either the atypicals or the neuroleptics because increasing the dose does not seem to help decrease the symptoms of schizophrenia but does increase the occurrence of side effects. In addition, many patients may suffer from depression, so doctors will prescribe additional medications to treat this. It is important to watch out for interactions when the patient begins to take multiple medications. In addition, the doctor must be aware that many patients will self-medicate, using alcohol, tobacco, and prescription and illegal drugs to try to alleviate their symptoms. Some of these "medications" can interfere with the action of the antipsychotic medications, often making them less effective.[9]

Therapy

Most people who are diagnosed with schizophrenia find themselves frightened, as do their families and friends. They are not sure how they will be able to handle day-to-day things anymore and do not know if they can overcome their disorganized thinking. This is where the therapist takes over. With schizophrenia, it is not enough to just take medication. Patients need to learn to understand their disorder and how to take care of their lives. Many feel that the education of the patient is second only to medication in preventing a relapse.

In general, a large number of patients, like Allison, find themselves hospitalized during their first psychotic episode. This is because family members may not know how to deal with them and also because doctors need a chance to work with the patient on a continual basis. While hospitalization may sound frightening, it can actually be the best thing for the patient who could be a danger to themselves or to others around them. Some patients say they feel safer in the hospital during a psychotic episode. However, some schizophrenia sufferers have no desire to be placed in a hospital and may end up there against their will. This is known as "being committed."

Hospital stays are usually quite brief, lasting less than a month. Private hospitals can be very expensive, while state run hospitals are cheaper. Currently, the standard of care in both may not be the same. State hospitals, while better than in earlier years, still have less money than those run by private corporations. The state-run hospital may not have new facilities and their caregivers are often paid less. This can result in a lower standard of care. However, many organizations are responsible for monitoring these institutions and the horror stories of the past do not occur as often. If possible, it is important to make sure that the patient is comfortable with the hospital that they are confined to because a positive experience will contribute toward their recovery.[10]

What to Do When the Patient Comes Home From the Hospital

It is difficult to know how to treat the patient when they come home from the hospital. Many families will feel sad and disappointed. The patient may feel depressed or be in denial about his or her diagnosis. He or she may feel better, but not be completely well. Time is needed to get used to new medications. Often, doctors start the patient on a dose of medication that may be too high for them, to help them get over their crisis. The side effects that show up from these high doses will disappear once the patient is prescribed a lower dosage.[11]

More than likely, the patient will be angry and withdrawn. He or she may get angry with their family members and yell at them. The patient may still hear voices for a while because this symptom is slow to go away, even with medication. He or she may feel stupid and frustrated. The medications can make the patient drowsy and want to sleep a lot. There is a tendency for newly diagnosed patients to gain weight and not exercise. The patient may not care about their physical appearance or want to bathe.[12]

These are difficult things for families to adjust to. Many experts say that the patient's environment should be very calm, with few upsets or activities and little expression of emotion. The parents should give the patient a little extra consideration. They should not have heart-to-heart talks with them or ask them a lot of questions. It is important to include them in daily activities but to expect that they will probably not want to participate right away. Many parents have started slowly by suggesting that the schizophrenia sufferer begin to do some simple household chores. This will help ready them to go back to school or work in the future. The family should also gradually work toward leaving the patient home alone and encourage independence. In addition, some patients may want to visit those they met while in the hospital. This should be encouraged because talking to other people who suffer from schizophrenia may be helpful to the newly diagnosed patient.[13]

The general atmosphere for the patient should be one of quiet activities and loving support. This may be hard for the caregiver, who should try to continue to maintain a normal life. Many programs exist that offer support to families during the patient's initial return to the household.

In the first months after diagnosis, most therapy is very intense, often occurring daily with both the patient and their family. These sessions address the depression, anger, and fear that the schizophrenia sufferer may be facing. Parents and spouses need to educate themselves because they are usually the major caregivers. Most sufferers do not spend very much time in hospitals, but instead live with their families or eventually on their own.

After being stabilized on medications and completing basic educational therapy, the patient may start a vocational or day-care program. These programs teach the patient some coping skills, such as dealing with money, holding a job, and maintaining an apartment and relationships. Schizophrenia

Therapy is an integral part of the treatment for schizophrenia.

sufferers deal with very disordered thinking, so these tasks may be very difficult. Therapists work to build a pattern for the patient to follow. Some of the vocational programs will find jobs for the schizophrenia sufferer, starting them in positions of low responsibility and helping them to move into more complex and demanding areas. In a general sense, therapy for the schizophrenia sufferer is very practical, focusing on the "here and now" and not on the past. Because it is a lifelong treatment, some therapists try many different approaches, including music, art, group, and recreational therapy. Each patient may respond in distinct ways so, like medication, therapy is a process of trial and error.[14]

Currently, there is much controversy over how to handle the diagnosis of schizophrenia. Some therapists feel that the disease is so frightening that patients should not be told. Because there are no definitive tests, such as a blood or genetic test, and because the diagnosis can be so devastating, a large number of therapists do not feel the need to tell their patients that they have schizophrenia. In contrast, many feel that this is the wrong approach. They state that if the patient does not understand his or her disease, then he or she may never adjust to his or her condition. Someone who does not know the course of the illness may not continue to take medication or to see a therapist and will most likely suffer another psychotic episode. At this stage, many who are not told that they have schizophrenia initially find out later, when visiting another doctor.

Mainly, the responsibilities of the doctors who treat those with schizophrenia are to keep their patients on medication, guide them through their day-to-day living, and help to prevent a recurrence of symptoms. While this sounds simple, it can be a very difficult task and much of the responsibility lies with the patient. Only those who want to feel better will.

6

Social Implications of Schizophrenia

Starting in the 1950s and increasingly in the late 1970s, mental health authorities and politicians decided that it might be best to begin a program that involved deinstitutionalizing the mentally ill. *Deinstitutionalization* involved assessing the progress of patients and releasing those who were able to live on their own. The plan was to provide outpatient services to help those living on their own manage their illness. Health care experts felt that this would save money because many people in institutions were not paying for the services, but were instead in state hospitals.

In some cases, this approach worked very well for patients who could organize their lives and manage to see their doctors, go to the outpatient support programs, and keep appointments. But schizophrenia is a disease that causes disordered thinking. Many schizophrenia sufferers who were released from hospitals never went back to a doctor. It is estimated that about 50 percent of the patients released during this time stopped taking their medications when they left the hospital. Without any guidance or a place to live, many of these patients found themselves with nowhere to go. This led to an increase in the number of homeless people on the streets of America's towns and cities. Authorities say that well over a third of the homeless population and those found in overnight shelters suffer from schizophrenia. The majority of homeless people in our country do not suffer from schizophrenia, but instead battle with addictions and other mental disorders. For many reasons, these people do better on the streets than do sufferers of schizophrenia.[1]

The trend to deinstitutionalize continued at an alarming rate. By the early 1980s, people suffering from schizophrenia were being released from hospitals in large numbers. Some had families who did not want to take care of them or did not know how. Before in large cities, it was common to find cheap boarding houses in the less desirable neighborhoods, but because the cities were becoming popular places to live, many of those neighborhoods were becoming more populated, and the cost to live in those areas rose. This forced boarding houses to close, leaving many schizophrenia sufferers with no place to stay except overnight shelters and on the streets. A federal task force commissioned to study the homeless with severe mental illness estimated that only 5 to 7 percent needed to be permanently institutionalized. Most, the task force said, could do fine in community-based treatment services, but many places do not have community-based treatment plans. As a result, people suffering from schizophrenia often fell through the cracks.[2]

Because schizophrenia can produce a disorganized way of thinking, the homeless schizophrenia sufferer does not generally fare well. The streets are mentally challenging and can pose difficulties even for those without mental illness. People suffering from schizophrenia are less able to survive and are usually bewildered. This contributes to high levels of depression and anxiety and, as a result, schizophrenia sufferers are more likely to commit suicide and acts of violence.[3]

Within the homeless schizophrenia-sufferer communities, there are many unexplained deaths. Because they are so overwhelmed by the life on the street, they may attempt to deal with the pain and uncertainty by drinking alcohol. They are more prone to drug use and display the diseases that go along with that, such as HIV (human immunodeficiency virus), at a higher rate than usual. The female homeless schizophrenia sufferer is raped more often than other women, including other homeless women. The lack of understanding of the culture of life on the street makes the sufferer a target.[4]

We often call these people bums or street people, and in general no one really knows what to do about them. Those with schizophrenia generally do not want contact with authorities, so they do not seek help, but instead remain isolated. They experience a lot of anxiety and suffering without any relief. They can usually find food and shelter for the night, but many are reluctant to do so and will only come into the shelters when it is very cold. The schizophrenia sufferer on the street can be a difficult person with which to deal. Sometimes they are very vocal, walking through the streets yelling. Many people find this frightening and disturbing. Others see the sufferer as a potential victim, someone to tease or abuse. While there are some programs to help the homeless schizophrenia sufferer, in general our society is passive, and many say these people are on the street because they want to be. In reality, they are on the street because they do not know how to manage their lives and may need more guidance than they are given. There does not appear to be an inexpensive way to solve this problem, so it is likely to continue for some time.[5]

Schizophrenia is an expensive disease. In the United States alone, billions of dollars are spent annually on treatment programs, hospitalization, and research.[6] As much money is spent on programs to help the schizophrenia sufferer as is spent on heart disease in the United States, and more than is spent on diabetes, but the costs are not taken care of by managed health care organizations as readily as the other two diseases. Instead, in schizophrenia-related cases, the government pays expenses. In addition, there is the loss of wages because many of those who have schizophrenia cannot hold a job. Many end up on disability, which can be especially devastating to the nation's annual budget because many of these people are young and may end up collecting money for the rest of their lives.

Another expense is incurred by putting schizophrenia sufferers in jail. Eleven percent of males who suffer from schizophrenia have committed violent crimes,[7] usually due to

Some schizophrenia sufferers commit crimes, usually due to noncompliance with prescribed medication.

noncompliance with medication. Over one billion dollars is spent annually to house the schizophrenia sufferers in prison.[8] Prison life is severe, and those who best survive it must be socially perceptive. Schizophrenia sufferers in general do not do well with this and can end up being victimized or causing dissension among their fellow inmates. In addition, the people who care for prisoners do not always understand the disordered thinking of the mentally ill inmate. This can lead to frustration, and a prisoner with schizophrenia can become violent and incur more punishments than the average prisoner. They may be paroled less often and end up in prisons longer, extending the costs to the taxpayer.

Compeer

Compeer is a nonprofit organization that was started in Rochester, New York, in 1973. The program is based on the belief that a mentally ill person may have many health care providers, but what they also need is a friend. Compeer matches volunteers with people who have mental illness. The match can be between two adults, two children, or an adult and a child. The friend can help to prevent the loneliness, fear, isolation, and failure that a mentally ill person may experience. Each volunteer is asked to spend one hour a week with their match and to guarantee that they can do this for at least a year. The pair will be matched on what type of activities they enjoy. They may go out shopping, get some coffee, go to movies and concerts, or just throw a Frisbee around in the park. Many Compeer matches have lasted for more than ten years.

There are currently over 100 Compeer affiliates in the United States, Canada, and Australia. The organization is growing very quickly and its success has earned it many mental health care awards.

The economic burden is huge because people who suffer from schizophrenia cannot always maintain jobs. Many people think that good community support with vocational rehabilitation, crisis intervention, and education of the patient and family is the only way to decrease these costs, but these programs themselves can be expensive. Many states have instituted a program called PACT, which stands for Program for Assertive Community Treatment. PACT provides housing, transportation, counseling, and vocational training to the schizophrenia sufferer. It has team members who are trained in many disciplines, including psychiatry, psychology, social work, nursing, substance abuse, and vocational rehabilitation. This comprehensive approach was started in the 1960s, when mental health professionals noticed that the schizophrenia sufferer would make progress while in the hospital, but would regress when they went back out on their own.[9]

PACT teaches skills to people suffering from schizophrenia by placing them in volunteer positions within different businesses. The patient is not paid, but instead works for free and is supported by PACT. This gives the employer an incentive to train the schizophrenia sufferer because he does not have to pay him a wage. Getting back out into society helps the patient by raising self-esteem and increasing contact with the outside world. The schizophrenia sufferers in this program are less able to regress into their own thoughts and must now work on communicating with others, handling responsibility, and organizing their time. These jobs start out as very small, but the patient can gradually work up to more difficult tasks.

Eventually, PACT will help the schizophrenia sufferer find a permanent job and gain some financial independence. In addition, it promotes the continuance of education for the patient.

Because the first psychotic episode generally appears during a person's college years, many schizophrenia sufferers drop out of school. PACT has programs that allow the patient to return to school for free and to start slowly. Many of these people are highly intelligent and deserve to finish school, but their disorganized thinking makes it more difficult, often seemingly impossible.[10]

Those who participate with PACT spend less time in hospitals, are more often employed, have more independent living arrangements, and more positive social relationships than those who do not. It seems that these programs save money in the long run. The drawback is that they currently exist in only six states nationwide—Delaware, Indiana, Michigan, Rhode Island, Texas, and Wisconsin. Many in the mental health profession are pushing to see other states adopt the PACT approach. Aggressive community support appears to be beneficial for the patient and for the taxpayer.[11]

7

Current Research

The research that is currently being done to further the understanding of schizophrenia is very exciting. New developments are reported in the news almost daily, but the disease itself is still a big puzzle. This may be because the name schizophrenia does not refer to one disease but actually is a number of different diseases, all with a similar effect. Therefore, different groups of patients will result in different findings in research studies. No study yet has identified a trait that is present in all the schizophrenia sufferers studied. But the search continues.

Some of the current directions taken include:

Imaging of the Brain

Imaging the brains of schizophrenia sufferers is a very popular line of research. Some of the studies using imaging techniques are very ambitious, using large numbers of patients followed over many years. CAT (computerized axial tomography) scans and MRI (magnetic resonance imaging) images can show doctors the structures of the brain and allow them to measure the size and structure of certain parts to see any abnormalities. In a recent study, researchers found differences in the size of the large ventricles of the brain in those who had schizophrenia and in those who had just experienced their first psychotic episode.[1] In addition, MRI images have shown a decrease in gray matter and whole brain volume in some schizophrenia sufferers.[2]

PET (positron electron tomography) scans are also popular research tools. These techniques measure the amount of blood flow and heat in certain regions of the body. The technique is very popular with brain studies because it is so sensitive and can actually show doctors what part of the brain is being used and when. In a typical experiment, researchers will give the schizophrenia sufferer something to read or recite and then measure the blood flow in the different brain regions. What they find is that schizophrenia sufferers are less active in some brain areas and more active in others when compared to people who do not have the same disease performing the same task. The PET scan will have cool (green or blue areas) and warm (red or yellow areas) that correspond to areas of low and high activity.[3] Researchers feel that these differences may explain some of the disorganized thinking that is so common in schizophrenia sufferers.

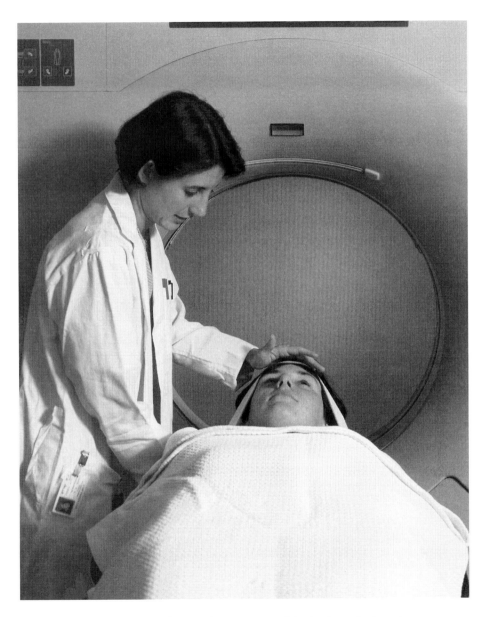

CAT scans can show doctors the structure of the brain and allow them to see any abnormalities that may exist.

Genetic Studies

Scientists are looking at the genes from families of schizophrenia sufferers to see if there is a pattern in the coding of the DNA that is similar for those with the disease but different in those without it. Genes are the regions in DNA that are read to make the proteins found in the body. Each gene codes for a different protein and sometimes they may code wrong. Most doctors realize that schizophrenia has many different forms and is probably caused by differences in an unknown number of genes. Recently, it was reported that a large percentage of schizophrenia sufferers have mutations in a gene on chromosome 22. This gene is expressed only in the brain. The protein it codes for is not known and is under investigation.[4]

Using DNA techniques, researchers have recently found that 28 percent of the schizophrenia sufferers that they studied had traces of a virus in their brains, suggesting that for some, schizophrenia may occur through an infection. The researchers looked at DNA from the brain and from spinal fluid, the liquid that surrounds the brain, of patients with schizophrenia. They then compared the DNA to those who did not have the disease. They find the virus hiding in the DNA, suggesting prior infection. Scientists call this viral DNA a "DNA footprint."[5] Whether this exact virus can cause the symptoms of schizophrenia is unknown.

Neurotransmitters

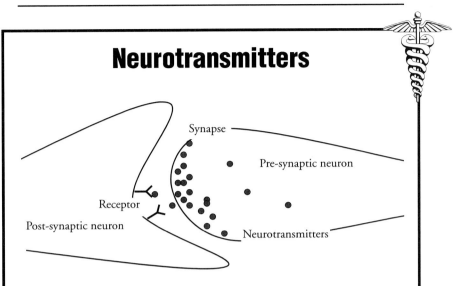

Signals are sent through the nerves in the brain by chemicals called neurotransmitters. The neurotransmitters are made and stored in the first nerve called the pre-synaptic nerve. When this nerve is excited by stimulation, the neurotransmitters are released and taken up by the post-synaptic nerve. The post-synaptic nerve will send a signal to another nerve or to muscles or organs. The space that the neurotransmitters are released into is called the synapse. Most post-synaptic nerves will have receptors on them that take up the neurotransmitter and bring it into the cell.

Some common neurotransmitters include:

- Acetylcholine
- Aspartate
- Dopamine
- Epinephrine
- Gamma aminobutyric acid (GABA)
- Glutamate
- Norepinephrine
- Serotonin

Social Studies

Current research is mainly focused on the social factors that could be one of the causes of schizophrenia. Many researchers want to find early clues for the disease because early treatment is associated with a positive outcome. The sooner the schizophrenia sufferer begins therapy and medication, the less chance there is of the patient experiencing the first psychotic episode. New research shows that there are signs in the patient that may appear three years before the onset of psychosis. These include some forms of disordered thinking and differences in brain images.[6] These studies are very important because many doctors feel that, in the early stages of schizophrenia, medications could stop the progression to psychosis. This would provide a better outcome for the patient.

Other researchers are working to destroy the myths of schizophrenia and give the patient new hope. Recent publications ask doctors to stop thinking "once a schizophrenia sufferer, always a schizophrenia sufferer." They are also being guided to stop thinking that all schizophrenic disorders are the same and that all patients respond to one treatment. Researchers are showing that psychotherapy, not just medication, does work, and that the patient benefits from this interaction even if it is not readily apparent. Another possible myth that is being challenged is that schizophrenia sufferers need to stay on their medication all of their lives. Doctors are being urged to wean patients from their medications if they seem to be more focused and organized and are not experiencing delusions.[7] This may be difficult for some doctors to do because there is an increase in the risk of suicide or violence in some patients when they are not taking their medication. There is a large amount of research dedicated to finding when it is safe to start to decrease the medications in patients.

In addition, much work is being done to find out how the family can help in the support of the patient with schizophrenia. Researchers are beginning to have a better understanding of what will make a patient noncompliant with their medications, which patient will have trouble with depression or substance abuse, and which will develop poor cognitive function. These findings can be relayed to the family. Research is showing that if the family is involved in the patient's care right away, the patient does better over time.

Drug Studies

The majority of the current research into schizophrenia is focused on designing new medications and making them safer for the patient. A lot of this work is being done at pharmaceutical companies. One of the more interesting approaches is designing a drug to work like nicotine in cigarettes. Research has shown that while about 25 to 30 percent of the adult population of the United States smokes, greater than 90 percent of schizophrenia sufferers do. Some have found that nicotine calms the sufferer and makes him or her more able to focus, but this is a brief phenomenon, lasting only a few minutes. In addition, cigarettes cause other diseases such as lung cancer and heart disease, so doctors want to see

A new approach to designing medication for schizophrenia sufferers is to make a drug that acts like nicotine in the brain. This new drug could help to calm the patient and alleviate some of the symptoms of schizophrenia.

their patients quit. Making a drug that acts like nicotine in the brain could help alleviate some of the symptoms of schizophrenia and calm the patient. An added bonus is that it could also help patients to quit smoking.[8]

Late-Onset Schizophrenia

Although most cases of schizophrenia occur in young adults, some patients develop the symptoms later in life. This is called *third age schizophrenia*, and research is showing that it is different from Alzheimer's disease and the senility that sometimes comes with aging. Many of the patients who develop schizophrenia later in life are women—the percentage being two to three times greater than men. They appear to do better on smaller doses of medications than those who develop the disease early, and their symptoms are less severe. Researchers feel that this type of schizophrenia may give a clue to what is happening in the younger brain.[9]

Other Causes

While much of the current research may seem strange, some findings could give clues to the different causes of schizophrenia. Recent work shows that schizophrenia occurs more often in left-handed people than in right-handed people. A large study was done using 3,000 college students who were chosen randomly. Those with schizophrenia and schizotypical disorders were more likely to be left-handed.[10] In addition, some schizophrenia sufferers appear to have a smaller number of ridges in their fingerprints. This may suggest a connection to something happening during fetal development.[11]

Some schizophrenia sufferers appear to have a decreased incidence of appendicitis and a decrease in platelets in the blood, the cells that help blood clot. No one knows what these differences mean, but they may point to a difference in the genes.[12] Another interesting approach is to study when schizophrenia sufferers are born in the year. It has been established that more schizophrenia sufferers are born during the winter months. Researchers have tried to determine if this has to do with changes in temperature during the seasons, or if it may have to do with how many older siblings the baby has. They have not yet found a connection. One study showed that more schizophrenia sufferers were born to mothers three months after the rainy season in tropical areas. This could support the idea that schizophrenia, in some cases, is caused by a virus—maybe one that flourishes during certain weather conditions. Perhaps the virus could be transmitted by a mosquito. More research is being done in this area and may yield some interesting results.[13]

Today's research into the causes of schizophrenia is going in many different directions. While most of the studies focus on medications, some are aimed at understanding the disease and the way it affects the body. Not many studies will come up with conclusive evidence of the cause or course of schizophrenia because it appears to be a disease with many different causes. But an increase in knowledge could help to make the patient's life more rewarding and less difficult.

Q&A

Q. What is schizophrenia?

A. Schizophrenia is a condition that is characterized by psychosis. The resulting inability to distinguish between reality and false information from their mind causes schizophrenia sufferers to adjust poorly to other people, and they often have trouble leading a normal life.

Q. What causes schizophrenia?

A. There are a number of factors that seem to predispose a person to schizophrenia. The biggest is heredity, but even identical twins only have a 50 percent chance of getting schizophrenia if their identical sibling has it. That is fifty times greater than the population at large, but if schizophrenia were totally genetic, the percent chance would be 100 percent. Other factors include exposure to viruses before birth, physical trauma before birth, different brain structure, and emotional stress. This variety of factors leads many to believe that schizophrenia is actually several illnesses that have the same symptoms.

Q. Are the parents at fault?

A. No. There is no evidence that anything the parents do after birth contributes to schizophrenia.

Q. Is schizophrenia "split personality?"

A. No. There is nothing in common between schizophrenia and multiple personality disorder. Perhaps this idea got started from the fact that schizophrenia means "split mind" in Latin.

Q. Can children develop schizophrenia?

A. Yes, but it is rare. Usually, people do not develop schizophrenia until they are older than fifteen, but it is possible for children as young as six years old to develop symptoms. While about one in 100 people get schizophrenia, only about one out of every 6,000 people under age twelve will have active symptoms.

Q. Is schizophrenia a new disease?

A. Although the name schizophrenia has only been used for about 100 years, accurate descriptions of the illness go back several thousand years, nearly to the beginning of written records. Presumably, some people suffered from schizophrenia even before that, but no written records were made.

Q. Are schizophrenia sufferers more likely to be violent?

A. Not usually; in general, people who suffer from schizophrenia are withdrawn and do not relate well to others. However, people who have paranoid schizophrenia can become violent; and in cases of illegal drug use, more schizophrenia sufferers can be violent.

Q. Do people who have schizophrenia get better?

A. Because schizophrenia appears to be mainly genetic, it never goes away. There also is no cure for it. On the positive side, though, many schizophrenia sufferers find that their symptoms fade after the age of forty-five, and 25 percent find that they no longer need medications.

Q. How long can schizophrenia sufferers expect to take antipsychotic medications?

A. Most schizophrenia sufferers should take their medications for their entire life. Not taking them will often result in further psychotic episodes that often cause damage to the person.

Q. Are there side effects to the medications?

A. Yes. The older antipsychotic medications were far worse, but even the atypical antipsychotic medications can cause side effects. The worst side effects can keep the patient from taking medications so it is very important to try to find the best possible medication for the patient.

Q. Will the future be better for schizophrenic treatments?

A. It should be. The past thirty years have shown more progress in treating schizophrenia than in the previous 3,000 years. There is every reason to expect better medications and therapy for treating the symptoms of schizophrenia.

Schizophrenia Timeline

1692—The Salem witch trials sentence nineteen people to death by hanging. Witchcraft and demonic possessions are common explanations for psychotic episodes.

1724—Cotton Mather, a Puritan clergyman, believes that mental diseases have physical causes and advances theories for explaining them. This goes against the prevailing theories of the time.

1792—The York Retreat for the mentally ill in England is founded by Quaker philanthropist and tea merchant William Tuke.

1807—Onset of a series of government-sponsored investigations into the appalling conditions of "madhouses" in England and elsewhere leads to widespread radical institutional reform and the building of new government-funded asylums.

1812—Benjamin Rush, one of the earliest advocates for the humane treatment of the mentally ill, establishes hospitals with improved living conditions for the mentally ill.

1903—Emil Kraepelin writes *Psychiatry: A Textbook for Students and Physicians*, which pulls back from the focus on brain-based mental illness and champions a new focus on systematic, longitudinal diagnosis and classification. He describes the two major psychoses of twentieth-century psychiatry: dementia praecox and manic depression.

1908—Clifford Beers writes *The Mind that Found Itself*, a patient testimonial of life inside an asylum that helped launch the mental hygiene movement

1924—Eugen Bleuler updates Kraepelin's division of the psychoses into dementia praecox and manic-depressive varieties by supplanting the former with a more comprehensive category of schizophrenia.

1933—Manfred Sakel introduces insulin shock therapy, which is used for a short time as a treatment for schizophrenia. Insulin shock therapy induces a temporary coma and often harms patients.

1935—Ladislav Meduna introduces Metrazol (cardiazol) convulsive shock therapy.

1935—In Portugal, Egas Moniz carries out the first frontal lobe psychosurgery operations, which he calls "frontal lobe leucotomies."

1938—In Italy, Cerletti and Bini introduce electroconvulsive shock therapy. While originally a treatment for schizophrenia, it will later be found to be much more effective for depression.

1940s—Electrotherapy is first used in hospitals in the United States as a treatment for mental illness.

1946—The United States government establishes the National Institute of Mental Health (NIMH).

1952—The first *Diagnostic and Statistical Manual* (DSM-I) is published in response to the demonstration that 90 percent of the cases filling hospitals were unclassifiable using *Standard Classified Nomenclature of Disease* mental illness diagnostic categories.

1952—First documented use of chlorpromazine by French psychiatrists Delay, Deniker, and Harl as an "anti-psychotic" for schizophrenia.

1954—The Food and Drug Administration approves use of chlorpromazine (brand name Thorazine) as the first antipsychotic medication in American psychiatry; many variations follow.

1970—Lithium is approved as a treatment for bipolar (manic-depressive) disorder in the United States.

1970s–early 1980s—Deinstitutionalization, or the act of releasing the mentally ill to community programs, or the streets, begins.

1980—Robert Spitzer leads the way in producing the DSM-III, which rids the field of psychiatry of its pre-formed, rigid ways of diagnosing mental illness. The new guidelines allow for more overlap and describe additional symptoms for each disorder.

1994—The DSM-IV, the largest *Diagnostic and Statistical Manual* to date, is published. It includes nearly 300 diagnostic categories.

1994—The atypical antipsychotic medications are introduced.

Glossary

affect—A person's mood. Doctors commonly talk about a "flat affect," which means no mood at all.

affective disorders—Mental illness characterized by greatly exaggerated emotional reactions and mood swings, from very happy to deeply sad.

anxiety—Fear and nervousness, usually for no reason.

bipolar (manic-depressive) disorder—A type of mental disorder in which patients go through two types of extreme moods, usually in a short time period. They may experience episodes of mania (happy, excited, nervous, very active) and then episodes of depression (sad, disinterested, inactive).

cerebral cortex—The outermost layer of the two hemispheres (halves) of the brain, which is responsible for all forms of conscious experience, including perception, emotion, thought, and planning.

chromosome—The storage site for DNA. Chromosomes are found in the nucleus, or "brain," of the cell.

chronic—Occurring over a long period of time.

debilitating—Altering every aspect of life; changing how a person functions in his or her daily life.

delusion—A fixed belief that is not true. People suffering from this type of thought disorder may be convinced that they are famous, are being followed by someone, or are capable of great things.

depression—A disorder characterized by a profound and persistent sadness.

derangement—Disordered; not functioning in a normal way.

diagnosis—Determining what disease a person has by studying their signs and symptoms.

dopamine—A neurotransmitter known to have multiple functions depending on where it acts in the brain. It is thought to control emotional responses and play a role in schizophrenia.

frontal lobe—One of the four divisions of each hemisphere of the cerebral cortex in the brain. The frontal lobe controls movement and organizes the functions of other parts of the brain.

gene—Located on a chromosome, a gene is an arrangement of DNA that is used to direct ("code" for) the making of proteins.

hallucination—An abnormal sensory experience that happens without any outside stimulation. Hallucinations may be auditory (hearing imaginary voices or music), visual (seeing something that is not there), tactile (feeling things that are not there), olfactory (smelling odors that do not exist) and taste (tasting something when nothing is there). Most hallucinations are auditory or visual.

mania—A mental disorder characterized by excessive excitement, happy feelings, and hyperactivity.

neologism—An invented word that normally does not exist. Schizophrenia sufferers may use neologisms often because their thoughts are disorganized.

neural network—A type of computer or computer program that uses logical connections that are less linear and more like the human brain.

neuron—The cell that makes up the nerves. Neurons communicate with one another and are characterized by long, fibrous projections called axons, and shorter, branchlike projections called dendrites. The neurotransmitters are released from and picked up by neurons.

neurosis—An emotional disturbance in which the patient's behavior and thinking are poorly adapted and cause suffering.

neurotransmitter—A chemical that is released by a nerve to cause a reaction or stop a reaction in another nerve or muscle cell.

obsession—A strange thought that keeps coming up in a person's mind, despite the knowledge that it is pointless or senseless. Obsessions may be accompanied by compulsive behaviors that serve to reduce the associated anxiety.

prevalent—Common; frequent.

progressive—Following a predicted course of changes. Progressive diseases, such as cancer, will continue to get worse with time.

psychiatrist—A licensed physician who specializes in mental illness. Training involves a medical degree (M.D.) and a four-year residency (more training). Psychiatrists will give patients therapy and can prescribe medications.

psychiatry—The medical science that deals with the origin, diagnosis, prevention, and treatment of mental and emotional diseases.

psychoanalysis—A type of therapy introduced by Dr. Sigmund Freud which involves talking to a doctor about dreams and childhood experiences to overcome current problems. The therapy is based on the thought that we behave the way we do because of things that happened to us when we were young.

psychologist—A person who holds a doctorate (Ph.D.) in psychology from an accredited school. Psychologists involved with patient care are called clinical psychologists. The psychologist provides psychotherapy but is not licensed to prescribe medicine because they are not medical doctors.

psychology—A science dealing with the study of the mental processes and behavior of people and animals.

psychosis—A major mental disorder in which a person's ability to think, respond emotionally, remember, communicate, interpret reality, and behave appropriately is so impaired that they cannot function and meet the ordinary demands of life.

psychosomatic illness—An illness that is caused by the mind that causes the body to experience symptoms.

psychotherapy—The treatment of a patient's mental and emotional problems through conversations between patient and therapist.

reuptake—A process by which released neurotransmitters are taken back up by the cell that released them so they can be used again.

schizophrenia—Severe and often chronic brain disease that includes symptoms such as personality changes, withdrawal, thought and speech disturbances, hallucinations, delusions, and bizarre behavior.

stigma—A term indicating an individual's noticeable features—either physical or behavioral—or non-noticeable features, that lead to social rejection.

synapse—A tiny gap between two nerve cells (neurons) that functions as the site where neurotransmitters are exchanged.

tardive dyskinesia—An abnormal involuntary movement disorder caused by some medications used to treat schizophrenia. Patients with tardive dyskinesia may smack their lips, have unwanted mouth movements, make faces, have involuntary bending at the waist, and have wiggling knees.

temporal lobe—One of the four major subdivisions of each hemisphere of the cerebral cortex in the brain. It functions in hearing, speech and sight.

For More Information

American Psychiatric Association (APA)
1400 K Street N.W.
Washington, DC 20005
(888) 357-7924
http://www.psych.org

National Alliance for Research on Schizophrenia and
Depression (NARSAD)
60 Cutter Mill Road, Suite 404
Great Neck, NY 11021
(800) 829-8289
http://www.mhsource.com/narsad

National Mental Health Association (NMHA)
1021 Prince Street
Alexandria, VA 22314
(800) 969-6642
http://www.nmha.org

World Fellowship for Schizophrenia and Allied Disorders
(WFSAD)
869 Yonge Street, Suite 104
Toronto, Ontario M4W 2H2 Canada
(416) 961-2855
http://www.world-schizophrenia.org

Chapter Notes

Chapter 1. Schizophrenia: The Monster That Steals Youth

1. I. Chovil, "The Experience of Schizophrenia," n.d., <http://www.chovil.com> (June 1, 2002).

2. Ibid.

3. Ibid.

4. Ibid.

5. Ibid.

6. Ibid.

7. A. R. Yung and P. D. McGorgy, "The Prodromal Phase of First Episode Psychosis: Past and Current Conceptualizations," *Schizophrenia Bulletin*, vol. 22 (2), 1996, pp. 353–370.

Chapter 2. History

1. C. Sullivan, "In a Nutshell: History of Mental Illness," n.d., <http://www.i5ive.com/article.cfm/mental_health/24473> (June 5, 2002).

2. Ibid.

3. "A Brilliant Madness," n.d., <http://www.pbs.org/wgbh/amex/nash/timeline/> June 5, 2002).

4. R. Walters, "A Brief History of Schizophrenia," n.d., <http://www.cellscience.com/shdss2.html> (May 22, 2001).

5. Sullivan (May 31, 2002).

6. Ibid.

7. Walters.

8. "Dorthea Dix," n.d., <http://www.humboldt1.com/~history/rogerson/dorthea.htm> (May 30, 2002).

9. H. Fabrega, Jr., "Culture and History of Psychiatric Diagnosis and Practice," *Psychiatric Clinics of North America*, September 24, 2001, Vol. 3, pp. 391–405.

10. Sullivan.

11. T. A. Ban, "Pharmacotherapy of Mental Illness: A Historical Analysis," *Progress in Neuropsychopharmacology and Biological Psychiatry*, May 25, 2001, Vol. 4, pp. 709–727.

12. "Prozac Makes History," n.d., <http://www.prozac.com/HowProzacCanHelp/ProzacMakesHistory.jsp> (May 30, 2002).

Chapter 3. What is Schizophrenia?

1. American Psychiatric Association, *Diagnostic and Statistical Manual of Mental Disorders*, Fourth Edition, Text Revision (Washington, D.C.: American Psychiatric Association, 2000), p. 312.

2. The Schizophrenia Homepage, "Roots of Schizophrenia May Lie in Development of Fetal Brain," n.d., <http://www.schizophrenia.com/news/causes2.html> (May 27, 2001).

3. E. F. Torrey, "Prevalence studies in schizophrenia," *British Journal of Psychiatry*, Vol. 150, 1987, pp. 598–608.

4. National Institute of Health, *NIH Publication No. 99-3517*, 1999, p. 9.

5. R. M. Murray and P. McGuffin, "Genetic Aspects of Psychiatric Disorders," R. E. Kendall and A. K. Zealley, ed., *Companion to Psychiatric Studies*, Fifth Edition (Edinburgh: Churchill-Livingstone, 1993), pp. 227–261.

6. T. F. McNeil, "Perinatal Risk Factors and Schizophrenic: Selective Review and Methodological Concerns," *Epidemiol Review*, Vol. 17, 1995, pp. 107–112.

7. E. S. Susser, "Schizophrenia After Prenatal Exposure to the Dutch Hunger Winter of 1944–1945," *Archives of General Psychiatry*, Vol. 49, 1992, pp. 983–988.

8. J. McGrath and R. Murray, "Risk Factors for Schizophrenics: From Conception to Birth," S. R. Hirsch and D. R. Weinberger, ed., *Schizophrenia* (Oxford: Blackwell Science, 1995), pp. 187–205.

9. P. J. Taylor, "Schizophrenia and the Risk of Violence," S. R. Hirsch and D. R. Weinberger, ed., *Schizophrenia* (Oxford: Blackwell Science, 1995), pp. 163–183.

10. P. J. Taylor, M. Leese, and D. Williams, "Mental Disorder and Violence: A Special (High Security) Hospital Study," *British Journal of Psychiatry*, Vol. 172, 1998, pp. 218–226.

Chapter 4. Diagnosing Schizophrenia

1. American Psychiatric Association, *Diagnostic and Statistical Manual of Mental Disorders,* Fourth Edition, Text Revision (Washington, D.C.: American Psychiatric Association, 2000), p. 303.

2. C. Bowles, "Diagnosing schizophrenia: An artificial brain aims to pick up early signs of schizophrenia," *New Scientist*, Vol. 24, February 2001, p. 117.

3. Ibid.

4. I. Chovil, "Early Intervention," n.d., <http://www.chovil.com/fpep.html>, (July 6, 2001).

5. T. Ilani, D. Ben-Shachar, R. D. Strous, M. Mazor, A. Sheinkman, M. Kotler, and S. Fuchs, "A Peripheral Marker for Schizophrenia: Increased Levels of D3 Dopamine Receptor mRNA in Blood Lymphocytes," *Proceedings of the National Academy of Science*, Vol. 98, January 16, 2001, pp. 625–628.

6. Ibid.

7. E. L. Goldman, "Do Not Wait to Treat Schizophrenic Patients: Long-Term Benefits Outweigh Side Effects," *Clinical Psychiatry News*, July 1996, p. 5.

8. B. Green, "A Review of Schizophrenia," n.d., <http://www.priory.com/schizo.htm> (June 4, 2001).

Chapter 5. Treatment of Schizophrenia

1. P. J. Weiden, "Expert Consensus Treatment Guidelines for Schizophrenia: A Guide for Patients and Families," *Journal of Clinical Psychiatry*, Vol. 60, 1999, pp. 1–8.

2. Ibid.

3. Ibid.

4. J. McGrath and W. B. Emerson, "Treatment of Schizophrenia," *British Medical Journal,* October 16, 1999, pp. 1045–1048.

5. J. F. Thornton, et al., "Schizophrenia: The Medications," n.d., <http://www.mentalhealth.com/book/p42-sc3.html> (June 1, 2002).

6. "Sane Line: Medical Methods of Treatment," n.d., <http://www.sane.org.uk//About_Mental_Illness/Medical_Treatments.htm> (June 1, 2002).

7. Ibid.

8. Ibid.

9. M. K. Spearing, "Schizophrenia," NIH Publication No. 99-3517, 1999, unpaged.

10. "Introduction to Schizophrenia," n.d., <http://www.schizophrenia.com/family/schizintro.html> (June 1, 2002).

11. Ibid.

12. Ibid.

13. Ibid.

14. Ibid.

Chapter 6. Social Implications of Schizophrenia

1. The Schizophrenia Society of Seskatchewan, "Recognizing Schizophrenia For What It Really Is: Many People With Schizophrenia Are Homeless," n.d., <http://www.t2.net/schsak/recognise3.htm> (May 30, 2002).

2. R. G. Krieg, "An Interdisciplinary Look at the Deinstitutionalization of the Mentally Ill," *The Social Science Journal,* Vol. 38, 2001, pp. 367–380.

3. "Poor Treatment = Increased Criminality," *Prelapse Magazine,* No. 2, September 1995, <http://www.mentalhealth.com/mag1/pre-poor.html> (June 1, 2002).

4. The Treatment Advocacy Center, "Briefing Paper; Victimization: One of the Consequences of Failure to Treat," n.d., <http://www.psychlaws.org/BriefingPapers/BP5.htm> (May 29, 2002).

5. Krieg.

6. "U.S. Health Official Puts Schizophrenia Costs at $65 Billion," n.d., <http://www.schizophrenia.com/news/costs1.html> (May 29, 2002).

7. E. F. Torrey, "Community Care and Schizophrenia," *The Lancet*, May 20, 2000, pp. 1827–1828.

8. "New Study Shows That Medications Keep Mentally Ill Out of Jail," n.d., <http://www.schizophrenia.com/newsletter/996/996jail.htm> (June 1, 2002).

9. R. Cowdry, "Schizophrenia," n.d., <http://www.nami.org/helpline/schizophrenia.htm> (May 30, 2002).

10. J. Frey and J. Bradshaw-Rouse, "Serving Teens With Assertive Community Treatment," n.d., <http://www.nami.org/youth/PACTeens.html> (June 1, 2002).

11. Cowdry.

Chapter 7. Current Research

1. D. Fannon, X. Chitnis, V. Doku, L. Tennakoon, and S. O'Ceallaigh, et al., "Features of Structural Brain Abnormality Detected in First-Episode Psychosis," *American Journal of Psychiatry*, Vol. 157, 2000, pp. 1829–1834.

2. Ibid.

3. R. Sabbatini," The PET Scan: A New Window Into the Brain," n.d., <http://www.epub.org.br/cm/n01/pet/pet.htm> (June 1, 2002).

4. K. P. Lesch, "Hallucinations: Psychopathology Meets Functional Genomics," *Molecular Psychiatry*, (4) July 3, 1998, pp. 278–281.

5. H. Karlsson, S. Bachman, J. Schroder, J. MacArthur, E. F. Torrey, and R. H. Yolken, "Retroviral RNA Identified in Cerebrospinal Fluids and Brains of Individuals With Schizophrenia," *Proceedings of the National Academy of Science*, April 10, 1998, pp. 4634–4639.

6. O. Guralnik, "Schizophrenia: The Rationale for Early Detection and Intervention," n.d., <http://www.schizophrenia.com/news/earlydet.html> (June 1, 2002).

7. National Institute of Mental Health, "Schizophrenia—How It Is Treated," n.d., <http://www.nimh.nih.gov/publicat/schizoph. htm#schiz3> (June 1, 2002).

8. S. Leonard, C. Breese, C. Adams, and C. Benhamnouk, "Smoking and Schizophrenia: Abnormal Nicotinic Receptor Expression," *European Journal of Pharmacology*, March 30, 2000, pp. 237–242.

9. D. V. Jeste, L. L. Symonds, M. J. Harris, et al., "Nondementia Nonpraecox Dementia Praecox?: Late-onset Schizophrenia," *American Journal of Geriatric Psychiatry*, Vol. 5, (4), 1997, pp. 302–317; and J. B. Lohr, M. Alder, and K. Flynn, et al., "Minor Physical Anomalies in Older Patients With Late-onset Schizophrenia, Early-onset Schizophrenia, Depression, and Alzheimer's Disease." *American Journal of Geriatric Psychiatry*, Vol. 5 (4), 1997, pp. 318–323.

10. J. Shaw, G. Claridge, and K. Clark, "Schizotypy and the Shift From Dextrality: A Study of Handedness in a Large Non-clinical Sample," *Schizophrenia Research*, July 1, 2001, pp. 181–189.

11. P. Fearson, A. Lane, M. Aire, and J. Scannell, "Is Reduced Dermatoglyphic A-B Ridge Count a Reliable Marker of Developmental Impairment in Schizophrenia?" *Schizophrenia Research*, July 1, 2001, pp. 151–157.

12. K. Lazier, E. W. Chow, P. Abdel-Malik, L. E. Scutt, R. Weksberg, and A. S. Bassett, "Low Platelet Count in a 22q11 Deletion Syndrome Subtype of Schizophrenia," *Schizophrenia Research*, July 1, 2001, pp. 177–180; and H. Ewald, P. B. Mortensen, and O. Mors, "Decreased Risk of Acute Appendicitis in Patients With Schizophrenia or Manic-depressive Psychosis," *Schizophrenia Research*, April 30, 49(3):287–293.

13. E. L. De Messias, N. Ferreira Cordeiro, J. J. Coelho Sampaio, J. J. Bartko, and B. Kirkpatrick, "Schizophrenia and Season of Birth in Tropical Regions: Relationship to Rainfall." *Schizophrenia Research*, March 30, 2001, pp. 227–234.

Further Reading

Abramowitz, Mimi. *Schizophrenia.* Farmington Hills, Miss.: The Gale Group, 2001.

Carter, Rosalynn and Susan K. Golant. *Helping Someone with Mental Illness: A Compassionate Guide for Family, Friends and Caregivers.* New York: Times Books, Random House Publishers, 1998.

Meuser, Kim T. and Susan Gingerich. *Coping with Schizophrenia: A Guide for Families.* Oakland, Calif.: New Harbinger Publications, 1994.

Moe, Barbara. *Coping With Mental Illness.* New York: Rosen Publishing Group, Inc., 2001.

Roleff, Tamara L. and Laura K. Egendorf. *Mental Illness.* Farmington Hills, Miss.: The Gale Group, 2000.

Smith, Douglas W. *Schizophrenia.* Danbury, Conn.: Franklin Watts, 1993.

Internet Addresses

Compeer
Information on volunteering to partner with mentally ill patients.
  <http://www.compeer.org/1/n2.asp>

The Experience of Schizophrenia: Ian Chovil's Homepage
  <http://www.chovil.com>

The National Institute of Mental Health (NIMH)
A first stop for information on schizophrenia.
  <http://www.nimh.nih.gov/publicat/schizoph.htm>

Schizophrenia.com
A wide range of information and services for schizophrenia sufferers and their loved ones.
  <http://www.schizophrenia.com>

Index